TEST YOUR
SPANISH

Juan CÓRDOBA

Adapted for English speakers
by Elise Bradbury

Unit 1
ESENCIALES

Tema **Punctuation and spelling**

Select the translation with the correct punctuation.

1. Very good!

   Ⓐ ¡Muy bien!   Ⓑ Muy bien.   Ⓒ Muy bien!

2. True or false?

   Ⓐ Verdad o mentira?

   Ⓑ ¿Verdad o mentira.

   Ⓒ ¿Verdad o mentira?

   Answers page 10

3. Hello Laura, are you Spanish?

   Ⓐ ¿Hola, Laura, eres española?

   Ⓑ Hola, Laura, ¿eres española?

   Ⓒ Hola, Laura, eres española?

Select the translation with the correct spelling.

1. An attractive profession.

   Ⓐ Una bonita proffesión.   Ⓑ Una bonita profesión.

2. I'm a professor (*m.*).

   Ⓐ Soy professor.   Ⓑ Soy profesor.

3. Yes, okay.

   Ⓐ Sí, de accuerdo.   Ⓑ Sí, de acuerdo.

Tema **Greetings**

Choose the correct word to complete these greetings.

Answers page 10

1. Buenas ...

   Ⓐ noche.   Ⓑ noches.   Ⓒ nochas.

2. ... días.

   Ⓐ Buenas   Ⓑ Buen   Ⓒ Buenos

3. Buenas ...

Ⓐ tardes.   Ⓑ tarde.   Ⓒ tardos.

Tema **The verb *ser***

In these sentences, which pronoun is implied?

1. Es española.

Ⓐ Tú   Ⓑ Él   Ⓒ Ella

Answers page 10

2. Eres profesor.

Ⓐ Yo   Ⓑ Tú   Ⓒ Él

3. No soy guapo.

Ⓐ Yo   Ⓑ Tú   Ⓒ Ella

4. No es francés.

Ⓐ Yo   Ⓑ Él   Ⓒ Ella

Choose the correct verb to complete these sentences.

1. ... en Madrid.

Ⓐ Soy   Ⓑ Nací

2. ... Ibiza.

Ⓐ Eres   Ⓑ Eres de

3. ... español.

Ⓐ Es de   Ⓑ Es

4. ... de Nueva York.

Ⓐ Nací   Ⓑ Soy

5. ... París.

Ⓐ Soy   Ⓑ Soy de

Unit 1
ESENCIALES

Tema Verbs ending in *-ar* (first conjugation)

*Choose the most suitable reply to each question. The conversation uses the informal **tú**.*

Answers page 10

1. ¿Hablo bien español?

   Ⓐ Sí, habla bien español.　　Ⓒ Sí, hablas bien español.

   Ⓑ Sí, hablo bien español.

2. ¿Dónde trabaja la madre de Laura?

   Ⓐ Trabaja en Francia.　　Ⓒ Trabajo en Francia.

   Ⓑ Trabajas en Francia.

3. ¿Cómo te llamas?

   Ⓐ Se llama Juan.　　Ⓒ Me llamo Juan.

   Ⓑ Te llamas Juan.

4. ¿Estudias idiomas?

   Ⓐ Sí, estudia idiomas.　　Ⓒ Sí, estudias idiomas.

   Ⓑ Sí, estudio idiomas.

5. ¿Cómo me llamo?

   Ⓐ Te llamas Juan.　　Ⓒ Se llama Juan.

   Ⓑ Me llamo Juan.

Tema Masculine and feminine

Choose the correct adjective for each exclamation.

Answers page 10

1. ¡Qué ... idioma!

   Ⓐ bonito　　Ⓑ bonita

2. ¡Qué ... ciudad!

   Ⓐ bonito　　Ⓑ bonita

3. ¡Qué ... día!

Ⓐ bonito   Ⓑ bonita

4. ¡Qué ... nombre!

Ⓐ bonito   Ⓑ bonita

5. ¡Qué ... profesora!

Ⓐ buena   Ⓑ bueno

Tema   Adjectives of nationality

Choose the correct adjective for each context.

Answers
page 10

1. Gina es un nombre ...

Ⓐ italiano.   Ⓑ italiana.

2. Marsella es una ciudad ...

Ⓐ francés.   Ⓑ francesa.

3. Mi madre es ...

Ⓐ español.   Ⓑ española.

4. Mi profesora es ...

Ⓐ alemán.   Ⓑ alemana.

5. Franck es de Bruselas. Es ...

Ⓐ belgo.   Ⓑ belga.

6. El dólar es la moneda ...

Ⓐ estadounidense.   Ⓑ estadounidensa.

7. El profesor es...

Ⓐ chino.   Ⓑ china.

8. Lisboa es la capital...

Ⓐ portugués.   Ⓑ portuguesa.

Unit 1
ESENCIALES

Tema **Linking simple sentences**

Choose the correct coordinating conjunction for each sentence.

1. Hablo inglés ... no hablo alemán.

   Ⓐ y también   Ⓑ pero

x

Verbs

ser	*to be* (essential characteristics)
estudiar	*to study*
hablar	*to talk*
llamarse	*to be called* Note: in reflexive verbs, the reflexive pronoun is attached to the end of the infinitive.
nacer	*to be born* Note: **nací** (*I was born*) is the preterite tense.
trabajar	*to work*

The first three persons of the present tense

irregular verb	regular verbs ending in **-ar**	
ser	**hablar**	**llamarse**
soy	**hablo**	**me llamo**
eres	**hablas**	**te llamas**
es	**habla**	**se llama**

Words for questions and exclamations

These always have a written accent.

¡Qué...!	*What (a)... ! / How ...!*
¿Dónde...?	*Where... ?*
¿De dónde...?	*From where... ?*
¿Cómo...?	*How... ?*

Subject pronouns (singular)

yo	*I*
tú	*you* (informal singular)
él	*he, it* (m.)
ella	*she, it* (f.)

Unit 1
ÚTILES

Coordinating conjunctions

y	*and*
o	*or*
pero	*but*

Adverbs and adverbial phrases

sí	*yes*
no	*no*
de acuerdo	*okay, all right*
también	*also*
bien	*well*
muy bien	*very well*

Greetings

Hola	*Hello*
Buenos días	*Good morning* Note: used until after lunch
Buenas tardes	*Good afternoon / Good evening* Note: used in **la tarde** (*the afternoon*), from after lunch until night
Buenas noches	*Good night* Note: used at night, both for greeting someone at night and for wishing someone a good night

Languages and nationalities

As in English, the same term is used for a country's language and nationality, though in Spanish these are not capitalized and typically there are different forms for the person's gender (masculine or feminine).

alemán, alemana	*German* (m./f.)
belga	*Belgian* (m./f.)

chino/a	Chinese (m./f.)
español/a	Spanish (m./f.)
estadounidense	American (m./f.) (from the United States)
francés, francesa	French (m./f.)
inglés, inglesa	English (m./f.)
italiano/a	Italian (m./f.)
portugués, portuguesa	Portuguese (m./f.)

Nouns

el día	day
la tarde	afternoon, evening
la noche	night
el nombre	first name
el idioma	language
la madre	mother
la ciudad	city
la profesión	profession
el profesor	teacher, professor (m.)
la profesora	teacher, professor (f.)
la mentira	lie (untruth)
la verdad	truth, fact Note: the question **¿Verdad?** means Right? Isn't it?

Adjectives

| guapo/a | good-looking (m./f.) |
| **bonito/a** | attractive, pretty (m./f.) |

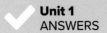

Unit 1
ANSWERS

ESENCIALES

PAGE 2
Punctuation and spellings
1 **A** 2 **C** 3 **B**
1 **B** 2 **B** 3 **B**

Greetings
1 **B** 2 **C** 3 **A**

PAGE 3
The verb *ser*
1 **C** 2 **B** 3 **A** 4 **B**
1 **B** 2 **B** 3 **B** 4 **B** 5 **B**

PAGE 4
Verbs ending in *-ar* (first conjugation)
1 **C** 2 **A** 3 **C** 4 **B** 5 **A**

Masculine and feminine
1 **A** 2 **B** 3 **A** 4 **B** 5 **A**

PAGE 5
Adjectives of nationality
1 **A** 2 **B** 3 **B** 4 **B** 5 **B** 6 **A** 7 **A** 8 **B**

PAGE 6
Linking simple sentences
1 **B** 2 **A** 3 **A** 4 **B** 5 **B**

Names
1 **C** 2 **B** 3 **C** 4 **A** 5 **A**

YOUR
SCORE:

Did you get between 0 and 8? ¡Ay, ay, ay! You're a bit rusty. Refresh your memory with a
level A2 course such as Assimil's *Target: Languages* and redo the questions.
Did you get between 9 and 17? Muy justito... You still got more wrong than right. Check
where your weak points are and review these in a course or reference book.
Did you get between 18 and 26? No está mal, pero... there is still room for improvement.
Analyse your mistakes (conjugation, grammar, vocabulary?) and focus on reviewing these
points.
Did you get between 27 and 35? Enhorabuena. You know the basics. Take your time:
you may be making mistakes by not paying attention.
Did you get 36 or over? ¡Eres un auténtico fenómeno! You're ready for the next level!

| **Tema** | **Word stress and written accents** |

Select where the word stress should go in the following words (indicated by the underlined syllable).

1. Madrid
   - Ⓐ <u>Ma</u>drid
   - Ⓑ Ma<u>drid</u>

2. mujer
   - Ⓐ <u>mu</u>jer
   - Ⓑ mu<u>jer</u>

3. edad
   - Ⓐ <u>e</u>dad
   - Ⓑ e<u>dad</u>

4. periodista
   - Ⓐ perio<u>dis</u>ta
   - Ⓑ periodis<u>ta</u>

5. comercio
   - Ⓐ co<u>mer</u>cio
   - Ⓑ comer<u>cio</u>

6. agricultor
   - Ⓐ agri<u>cul</u>tor
   - Ⓑ agricul<u>tor</u>

In the words below, does the accentuated syllable require a written accent?

1. [ale<u>man</u>]
   - Ⓐ aleman
   - Ⓑ alemán

2. [fran<u>cesa</u>]
   - Ⓐ francesa
   - Ⓑ francésa

3. [Pa<u>ris</u>]
   - Ⓐ Paris
   - Ⓑ París

4. [<u>Carmen</u>]
   - Ⓐ Cármen
   - Ⓑ Carmen

5. [<u>Angel</u>]
   - Ⓐ Ángel
   - Ⓑ Angel

6. [Or<u>tiz</u>]
   - Ⓐ Ortiz
   - Ⓑ Ortíz

Answers page 19

Tema	**Word stress and written accents**

Does the missing word in each sentence need a written accent?

1. La reina de España tiene dos hijas, ... yo.

   A como **B** cómo

   Answers page **19**

2. ... rey de España se llama Felipe.

   A El **B** Él

3. Yo soy funcionario, ¿y ...?

   A tu **B** tú

4. No estoy casada con ...

   A el. **B** él.

5. Y ... marido, ¿a qué se dedica?

   A tu **B** tú

6. Dime ... es vivir en Madrid.

   A como **B** cómo

Tema	**Counting to 100**

Select the missing number in each sequence.

Answers page **19**

1. cinco – diez – ¿? – veinte

   A cincuenta **B** quince **C** dieciséis

2. ¿? – veinticuatro – cuarenta y ocho – noventa y seis

   A ocho **B** dos **C** doce

3. ochenta y ocho – ¿? – veintidós – once

   A catorce **B** cuarenta y cuatro **C** treinta y cuatro

4. setenta y siete – sesenta y nueve – sesenta y uno – ¿?

   A cincuenta y tres **B** treinta y cinco **C** noventa y cinco

Tema Personal questions

Choose the most suitable response to each question.

1. ¿En qué trabajas?
   - (A) Juan Pérez López.
   - (C) Inglés y francés.
   - (B) Soy empleado.

   Answers page 19

2. ¿Qué edad tienes?
   - (A) Tengo treinta y ocho años.
   - (C) No, estoy desempleado.
   - (B) Tengo tres hijos.

3. ¿A qué te dedicas?
   - (A) En Madrid.
   - (C) Trabajo en la enseñanza.
   - (B) Sí, tengo un buen empleo.

4. ¿Cuántos años tienes?
   - (A) Setenta.
   - (C) No, no tengo trabajo.
   - (B) Dos, un hijo y una hija.

5. ¿Estás casado?
   - (A) Sí, tengo dos casas.
   - (C) Sí, y tengo dos hijas.
   - (B) Sí, soy ama de casa.

Tema *Ser* and *estar*

Choose the correct verb to complete each sentence.

Answers page 19

1. Letizia Ortiz ... la reina de España.
   - (A) es
   - (B) está

2. Tú ... Paco, ¿verdad?
   - (A) eres
   - (B) estás

3. ... casada con un profesor.
   - (A) Estoy
   - (B) Soy

4. No trabajas: ... desempleado.

    A eres   **B** estás

5. Tengo un buen trabajo: ... periodista.

    A soy   **B** estoy

Tema **The verbs *hacer*, *tener*, *ser*, *ver*, *vivir***

Choose the correct verb to complete these sentences.

1. ¿A cuántas preguntas ... derecho?

    A hago   **B** tengo

    Answers page 19

2. ¿Dónde ...?

    A vives   **B** haces

3. ¿Quién ...?

    A eres   **B** vives

4. ¿Qué ... tu marido?

    A está   **B** hace

5. ... tres casas.

    A Vivo   **B** Veo

6. ... en Sevilla.

    A Vive   **B** Ve

Tema **Some vocabulary**

Select the correct translation of each sentence.

1. I (m.) am married to a farmer (f.).

    Answers page 19

    A Estoy marido con una agricultora.

    B Soy marido con una agricultora.

    C Estoy casado con una agricultora.

2. My daughter is the same age as your son.

   (A) Mi hija tiene la edad de tu hijo.

   (B) Mi hija tiene el edad de tu hijo.

   (C) Mi hija tiene el año de tu hijo.

3. Tell me your family name.

   (A) Dime tu apellido.

   (B) Dime tu nombre.

   (C) Dime tu ama de casa.

Tema Masculine and feminine

Choose the correct article for each noun (sometimes both are correct).

1. rey

   (A) el   (B) la

   Answers page 19

2. periodista

   (A) un   (B) una

3. funcionario

   (A) un   (B) una

4. hija

   (A) el   (B) la

5. edad

   (A) el   (B) la

6. año

   (A) un   (B) una

7. mujer

   (A) un   (B) una

8. agricultora

   (A) el   (B) la

Unit 2
ESENCIALES

Tema Expressing delight or sympathy

Choose the appropriate reaction to each statement.

Answers page 19

1. Estoy desempleado.
   - **A** ¡Enhorabuena!
   - **B** ¡Qué lástima!

2. Tengo varias casas.
   - **A** ¡Enhorabuena!
   - **B** ¡Qué lástima!

3. Mi marido no tiene un buen empleo.
   - **A** ¡Enhorabuena!
   - **B** ¡Qué lástima!

4. Hablo diez idiomas.
   - **A** ¡Enhorabuena!
   - **B** ¡Qué lástima!

Verbs   ÚTILES

dedicarse a	*to devote oneself to, to do for a living*
estar	*to be* (locations and temporary states)
hacer	*to do, to make*
tener	*to have*
ver	*to see*
vivir	*to live*

Question words

¿Quién?	*Who?*
¿Cuántos...?	*How many...?* (+ masculine plural noun)
¿Cuántas...?	*How many...?* (+ feminine plural noun)

Work life

¿En qué trabajas?	*What area do you work in?*
¿A qué te dedicas?	*What do you do for a living?*
el trabajo	*work, job*

el empleo	*employment*
el desempleo	*unemployment*
desempleado/a	*unemployed* (m./f.)
funcionario/a	*civil servant, public employee* (m./f.)
agricultor/a	*farmer* (m./f.)
empleado/a	*employee* (m./f.)
periodista	*journalist* (m./f.)
una ama de casa	*housewife*
la enseñanza	*teaching*
el comercio	*commerce, trade, business*

Family

el hombre	*man*
el marido	*husband*
la mujer	*woman, wife*
el hijo / la hija	*son / daughter*
casado/a	*married* (m./f.)
estar casado/a con	*to be married to*

Name and age

el nombre	*first name*
el apellido	*family name* Note: in Spain, the family name consists of both parents' surnames.
la edad	*age*
el año	*year*
¿Qué edad tienes? / ¿Cuántos años tienes?	*How old are you?* (informal singular)
Tengo diez años.	*I'm ten years old.*

Unit 2
ÚTILES

Numbers to 100

*The numbers from 0 to 29 are written as a single word. From 30, the pattern is ten + **y** (and) + unit, in three separate words.*

0	**cero**	10	**diez**	20	**veinte**	30	**treinta**
1	**uno**	11	**once**	21	**veintiuno**	31	**treinta y uno**
2	**dos**	12	**doce**	22	**veintidós**	32	**treinta y dos**, etc.
3	**tres**	13	**trece**	23	**veintitrés**	40	**cuarenta**
4	**cuatro**	14	**catorce**	24	**veinticuatro**	50	**cincuenta**
5	**cinco**	15	**quince**	25	**veinticinco**	60	**sesenta**
6	**seis**	16	**dieciséis**	26	**veintiséis**	70	**setenta**
7	**siete**	17	**diecisiete**	27	**veintisiete**	80	**ochenta**
8	**ocho**	18	**dieciocho**	28	**veintiocho**	90	**noventa**
9	**nueve**	19	**diecinueve**	29	**veintinueve**	100	**cien**

Nouns and adjectives

el rey	*king*
la reina	*queen*
varios, varias	*several* (m./f.)
la pregunta	*question*
la casa	*house*
el derecho	*law, right, prerogative*

Expressions

¡Enhorabuena!	*Congratulations!*
¡Qué lástima!	*What a shame!*

ESENCIALES

PAGE 11

Word stress and written accents

1 **B** 2 **B** 3 **B** 4 **A** 5 **A** 6 **B**
1 **B** 2 **A** 3 **B** 4 **A** 5 **A** 6 **A**
1 **A** 2 **A** 3 **B** 4 **B** 5 **A** 6 **B**

PAGE 12

Counting to 100

1 **B** 2 **C** 3 **B** 4 **A**

PAGE 13

Personal questions

1 **B** 2 **A** 3 **C** 4 **A** 5 **C**

Ser and *estar*

1 **A** 2 **A** 3 **A** 4 **B** 5 **A**

PAGE 14

The verbs *hacer*, *tener*, *ser*, *ver*, *vivir*

1 **B** 2 **A** 3 **A** 4 **B** 5 **B** 6 **A**

Some vocabulary

1 **C** 2 **A** 3 **A**

PAGE 15

Masculine and feminine

1 **A** 2 **AB** 3 **A** 4 **B** 5 **B** 6 **A** 7 **B** 8 **B**

PAGE 16

Expressing delight or sympathy

1 **B** 2 **A** 3 **B** 4 **A**

YOUR SCORE:

Did you get between 0 and 10? ¡Ay, ay, ay!

Did you get between 11 and 21? Muy justito...

Did you get between 22 and 32? No está mal, pero...

Did you get between 33 and 43? Enhorabuena.

Did you get 44 or over? ¡Eres un auténtico fenómeno!

| Tema | **Meeting and greeting** |

Choose the most appropriate reply for each question or statement.

1. ¿Qué tal?

   Ⓐ Me alegro.   Ⓑ Regular, ¿y tú?   Ⓒ No.

   Answers page 28

2. Encantado.

   Ⓐ ¿Vale?   Ⓑ Sí.   Ⓒ Mucho gusto.

3. ¿Cómo estás?

   Ⓐ Fenomenal.   Ⓑ Muchas gracias.   Ⓒ De acuerdo.

Now choose the most likely question/statement that preceded each of these replies.

1. Muy mal.

   Ⓐ Ni fu ni fa.   Ⓒ Gracias.

   Ⓑ ¿Qué tal está tu madre?

2. ¡Hola, me alegro de verte!

   Ⓐ Bueno, vale.   Ⓒ ¡Muy bien!

   Ⓑ ¡Muy buenas!

3. Tanto gusto.

   Ⓐ Encantada.   Ⓒ Estoy fatal.

   Ⓑ ¿Estás bien?

| Tema | **Article–noun agreement** |

Select the correct form of the article 'the' in each context.

Answers page 28

1. ... profesores de matemáticas.

   Ⓐ Las   Ⓑ Los   Ⓒ La

2. ... delegada de clase.

   Ⓐ La   Ⓑ El   Ⓒ Las

3. ... buenas alumnas.

    A El   B Los   C Las

4. Están prohibidos ... chicles.

    A la   B los   C las

Complete each sentence with the correct pair of words.

Answers page 28

1. Soy ... enfermera ... instituto.

    A el / de el   B a las / del   C la / del

2. Veo ... amigas ... señora del Pino.

    A a las / de la   B las / dela   C los / de la

3. ¿Tienes ... número ... móvil de Pedro?

    A al / de la   B las / del   C el / de

4. Tengo ... móviles ... enfermeros.

    A a los / de las   B los / de los   C el / delos

Tema Subject and possessive pronouns

Choose the most suitable pronoun to complete each sentence.

Answers page 28

1. ¿Es ... nuevo móvil?

    A nosotros   B nuestro   C nuestra

2. ... son buenas alumnas.

    A Ellas   B Su   C Sus

3. ¿A qué tenéis derecho ... en el instituto?

    A vuestro   B vuestros   C vosotros

4. ... me alegro mucho de verte.

    A Mi   B Mis   C Yo

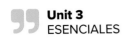

5. ¿Quiénes son ... delegados?

- A tú
- B tu
- C tus

6. Estoy casada con ...

- A él.
- B el.
- C su.

Tema **Informal and formal address**

Select the form of address used in each question or statement: ***tú*** *(informal) or* ***usted*** *(formal).*

1. ¿Cómo se llama?
   - A tú
   - B usted

Answers page 28

2. ¿De qué te alegras?
   - A tú
   - B usted

3. ¿Cómo está?
   - A tú
   - B usted

4. ¿Qué edad tiene?
   - A tú
   - B usted

5. Eres el bienvenido.
   - A tú
   - B usted

6. ¿Cuántos idiomas hablas?
   - A tú
   - B usted

In an informal conversation with a group of friends, which form of these questions would you use?

1. What do you (pl.) do for a living?
   - A ¿A qué os dedicáis?
   - B ¿A qué se dedican?

Answers page 28

2. Where do you (pl.) live?
   - A ¿Dónde vivís?
   - B ¿Dónde viven?

3. How are you (pl.)?

   A ¿Cómo están?   B ¿Cómo estáis?

4. Where are you (pl.) from?

   A ¿De dónde son?   B ¿De dónde sois?

In a formal conversation with someone in a more polite context, which form of these questions would you use?

1. Are you a nurse?

   A ¿Es enfermero?   C ¿Sois enfermeros? **Answers page 28**

   B ¿Eres enfermero?

2. How old are you?

   A ¿Cuántos años tenéis?   C ¿Cuántos años tienes?

   B ¿Cuántos años tiene?

3. Are you married?

   A ¿Estás casado?   C ¿Estáis casados?

   B ¿Está casado?

4. What field do you work in?

   A ¿En qué trabajáis?   C ¿En qué trabaja?

   B ¿En qué trabajas?

Tema Commands

Select whether each command addresses one person or more than one person.

1. ¡Hablad!

   A Speak! (singular)   B Speak! (plural) **Answers page 28**

2. ¡Trabaja!

   A Work! (singular)   B Work! (plural)

3. ¡Llámame!

(A) Call me! (singular)

(B) Call me! (plural)

4. ¡Tratadme de usted!

(A) Use **usted** with me! (sing.)

(B) Use **usted** with me! (pl.)

| Tema | **Some vocabulary and comprehension** |

Choose the correct translations.

1. We are not in a good mood.

(A) No somos de buena humor.

(B) No somos de buen humor.

(C) No estamos de buen humor.

Answers
page 28

2. On behalf of all of us, welcome.

(A) En nombre de todos, bienvenida.

(B) En nombre de otros, bienvenida.

(C) En nombre de los demás, bienvenida.

3. I'm sorry, it's not allowed.

(A) Entendido, está prohibido.

(B) Lo siento, está prohibido.

(C) Vale, está prohibido.

4. I'm not feeling well, so be quiet!

(A) No estoy bien, ¡ahora silencio!

(B) No estoy bien, pero ¡silencio!

(C) No estoy bien, ¡entonces silencio!

Verbs

alegrarse	*to be happy, to be glad*
tratar de tú / tutear	*to use the informal **tú***
tratar de usted	*to use the formal **usted***
prohibir	*to prohibit*

Saying and asking how things are

¿Qué tal?	*How is everything?* Note: this question can be used with **estar**, which conveys a reference to one's physical state or mood: **¿Qué tal estáis?** *How are you (pl.)?*
bien / muy bien	*fine, very well* Note: used with the verb **estar**: **Estoy bien.** *I'm well.*
fenomenal, divinamente, estupendamente	*fantastic, super, amazing*
mal, muy mal	*bad, very bad*
fatal	*terrible, awful*
regular	*so-so, not great*
ni fu ni fa	*neither good nor bad*
tirando	*bearing up, getting by*

Greetings

encantado/a	*pleased to meet you* (m./f.)
mucho gusto / tanto gusto	*pleased to meet you*
me alegro de verte	*I'm happy to see you*

Unit 3
ÚTILES

Polite address

usted / ustedes	*you* (formal sing./pl.) **Note:** the pronoun **usted** is used with the third-person singular verb: **¿Cómo se llama usted, señor?** *What's your name, sir?* The pronoun **ustedes** is used with the third-person plural verb: **¿Cómo se llaman ustedes, señores?** *What are your names, sirs?*
señor	*sir, Mr*
señora	*madam, Mrs*
señorita	*miss*
don Manuel, doña Carmen	*Mr Manuel, Mrs Carmen* **Note:** **don** and **doña** are respectful titles used before a first name, never directly before the family name.

Subject pronouns (plural)

nosotros/as	*we* (m./f.)
vosotros/as	*you* (m./f.) (informal plural)
ellos	*they* (m.)
ellas	*they* (f.)

Possessive adjectives

mi, mis	*my* (+ sing./pl. noun)
tu, tus	*your* (inf. sing.) (+ sing./pl. noun)
su, sus	*his, her, its* (+ sing./pl. noun)
nuestro/a, nuestros/as	*our* (+ m./f. sing., m./f. pl. noun)
vuestro/a, vuestros/as	*your* (inf. pl.) (+ m./f. sing., m./f. pl. noun)
su, sus	*their* (+ sing./pl. noun)

Expressions, adverbs and linking words

bienvenido/a	*welcome* (to a male/female)
gracias	*thank you*
muchas gracias	*thank you very much*
bueno	*good*
vale	*okay*
lo siento	*I'm sorry*
¿entendido?	*Got it? Understood?*
ahora	*now*
entonces	*then, so*

Nouns

delegado/a	*delegate, representative* (m./f.)
alumno/a	*student* (m./f.)
el instituto	*secondary school, high school*
el humor	*mood*
enfermero/a	*nurse* (m./f.)
el chicle	*chewing-gum*
el móvil	*mobile phone*
el silencio	*silence*

Pronouns and adjectives

todo/a, todos/as	*all, every* (m./f. sing., m./f. pl.)
otro/a, otros/as	*other* (m./f. sing., m./f. pl.)
los / las demás	*the others* (m./f.) Note: **los demás** refers to other people or objects within a group: **los demás alumnos del instituto** *the other high school students* / **los demás días de la semana** *the other days of the week.*

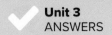

Unit 3
ANSWERS

ESENCIALES

PAGE 20

Meeting and greeting

1 **B** 2 **C** 3 **A**
1 **B** 2 **B** 3 **A**

Article–noun agreement

1 **B** 2 **A** 3 **C** 4 **B**
1 **C** 2 **A** 3 **C** 4 **B**

PAGE 21

Subject and possessive pronouns

1 **B** 2 **A** 3 **C** 4 **C** 5 **C** 6 **A**

PAGE 22

Informal and formal address

1 **B** 2 **A** 3 **B** 4 **B** 5 **A** 6 **A**
1 **A** 2 **A** 3 **B** 4 **B**
1 **A** 2 **B** 3 **B** 4 **C**

PAGE 23

Commands

1 **B** 2 **A** 3 **A** 4 **B**

PAGE 24

Some vocabulary and comprehension

1 **C** 2 **A** 3 **B** 4 **C**

YOUR SCORE:

Did you get between 0 and 9? ¡Ay, ay, ay!

Did you get between 10 and 17? Muy justito...

Did you get between 18 and 25? No está mal, pero...

Did you get between 26 and 33? Enhorabuena.

Did you get 34 or over? ¡Eres un auténtico fenómeno!

Tema Polite replies

Choose the appropriate polite reply in each situation.

1. ¿Puedes ayudarme?

   Ⓐ Por supuesto.   Ⓑ Gracias.   Ⓒ No hay de qué.

2. ¿Me invitas a un café?

   Ⓐ Perdón.   Ⓑ ¡De nada!   Ⓒ ¡Sí, claro!   **Answers page 37**

3. Muy amable.

   Ⓐ ¡De nada!   Ⓑ Lo siento.   Ⓒ Disculpa.

4. ¡Felicidades!

   Ⓐ Muchas gracias.   Ⓑ Por favor.   Ⓒ Fatal.

*One way of saying 'Excuse me ...' is **perdón** (pardon). Another is to use the verbs **perdonar** or **disculpar** (to pardon, to excuse). In that case, the verb needs to be in the appropriate formal or informal, singular or plural form. Select the correct verb form for each context.*

1. ..., ¿tenéis fuego?

   Ⓐ Disculpa   Ⓒ Disculpe   **Answers page 37**

   Ⓑ Disculpad   Ⓓ Disculpen

2. ..., ¿me puede hacer un favor?

   Ⓐ Disculpa   Ⓒ Disculpe

   Ⓑ Disculpad   Ⓓ Disculpen

3. ..., ¿me pasas el azúcar?

   Ⓐ Perdona   Ⓒ Perdone

   Ⓑ Perdonad   Ⓓ Perdonen

4. ..., me tratan de usted, ¿entendido?

   Ⓐ Perdona   Ⓒ Perdone

   Ⓑ Perdonad   Ⓓ Perdonen

Unit 4
ÚTILES

Adverbs and adverbial phrases

por supuesto	*of course*
claro que sí	*yes, certainly*
de nuevo	*again*
aquí	*here*
hay	*there is, there are*

Nouns

el azúcar	*sugar*
el café	*café, coffee*
el café con leche	*coffee with milk*
la cosa	*thing*
el hombre	*man*
la leche	*milk*
el vecino / la vecina	*neighbour* (m./f.)

Adjectives

poco/a	*few* (m./f.)
un poco de	*a few of*
pesado/a	*boring, tiresome, annoying* (m./f.)
amable	*kind, nice*

Direct object pronouns

<u>**Me**</u> **ve.**	*He sees* <u>*me*</u>.
<u>**Te**</u> **quiero.**	*I love* <u>*you*</u>.
<u>**Lo**</u> **/** <u>**la**</u> **ayudamos.**	*We help* <u>*him/her*</u>. (If the object is a person and is male, **le** can also be used.)
<u>**Nos**</u> **llamáis.**	*You* (pl.) *call* <u>*us*</u>.
<u>**Os**</u> **presento.**	*I introduce* <u>*you*</u> (pl.).
<u>**Los**</u> **/** <u>**las**</u> **molestas.**	*You're bothering* <u>*them*</u> (m./f.) (If the object refers to males, **les** can also be used.)

ESENCIALES

PAGE 29
Polite replies
1 **A** 2 **C** 3 **A** 4 **A**
1 **B** 2 **C** 3 **A** 4 **D**

PAGE 30
Informal and formal address
1 **B** 2 **C** 3 **A** 4 **B**
1 **B** 2 **C** 3 **A** 4 **C**
1 **B** 2 **A** 3 **A** 4 **C**
1 **B** 2 **C** 3 **A** 4 **B**

PAGE 32
The position of the object pronoun
1 **A** 2 **B** 3 **C** 4 **A**

PAGE 33
Articles and prepositions
1 **D** 2 **C** 3 **A** 4 **C**

Verbs with a spelling change
1 **C** 2 **A** 3 **B** 4 **C** 5 **A** 6 **B**

PAGE 34
Translation
1 **B** 2 **C** 3 **C** 4 **B** 5 **A**

YOUR
SCORE:

Did you get between 0 and 9? ¡Ay, ay, ay!

Did you get between 10 and 17? Muy justito...

Did you get between 18 and 25? No está mal, pero...

Did you get between 26 and 33? Enhorabuena.

Did you get 34 or over? ¡Eres un auténtico fenómeno!

| Tema | **Some vocabulary** |

Select the odd one out in these sets of words.

1.
- **A** el teléfono
- **B** el número
- **C** el nombre
- **D** el móvil

Answers page 46

2.
- **A** el apellido
- **B** el número
- **C** el nombre
- **D** María

3.
- **A** Adiós.
- **B** Hasta pronto.
- **C** Hasta la vista.
- **D** Dime.

4.
- **A** la dirección
- **B** Avda. de Madrid 31
- **C** Paseo de la Castellana 50
- **D** 112, dígame.

| Tema | **Addresses** |

Select the full word for each of these postal abbreviations of terms for streets.

Answers page 46

1. Pza.
- **A** piazza
- **B** plaza
- **C** plazza

2. C.
- **A** calle
- **B** cale
- **C** calla

3. Avda.
- **A** avenida
- **B** avenuda
- **C** avienida

4. Ctra.
- **A** cartera
- **B** carreta
- **C** carretera

Tema	**Telephone numbers**

Which number corresponds to the number written out in words?

Answers page 46

1. novecientos dos diecinueve cincuenta setenta y uno
   - (A) 9102195061
   - (B) 902195071
   - (C) 92119571

2. seiscientos sesenta treinta y siete doce noventa y seis
   - (A) 660371296
   - (B) 663072906
   - (C) 660307296

3. nueve cero uno veintinueve cuarenta y dos trece
   - (A) 90120940213
   - (B) 901294213
   - (C) 902194213

4. quinientos cinco cincuenta ochenta noventa
   - (A) 505508090
   - (B) 505058900
   - (C) 555080090

Tema	**Talking on the phone**

Choose the appropriate expression for each situation.

1. To answer the phone.
   - (A) ¿Pronto?
   - (B) Oiga.
   - (C) Diga.

2. To say that you're calling on behalf of someone.
   - (A) Llamo de parte de...
   - (B) Llamo de la parte de...
   - (C) Llamo por parte de...

   Answers page 46

3. To ask for Pedro, you could say **Quisiera hablar con Pedro**, or:
   - (A) ¿Me puede colgar con Pedro?
   - (B) ¿Me puede poner con Pedro?
   - (C) ¿Me puede llamar con Pedro?

4. To ask someone to hold/to stay on the line.
   - (A) No cuelgue.
   - (B) No se ponga.
   - (C) No me ponga.

5. To say goodbye, you could simply say **Adiós** or:
   - (A) Hasta adiós.
   - (B) Hasta luego.
   - (C) Hasta pronta.

Unit 5
ESENCIALES

Ser or *estar*? Choose the appropriate verb for each context.

1. To say 'It's me!'
   - Ⓐ ¡Soy!
   - Ⓑ ¡Soy yo!
   - Ⓒ ¡Estoy!

Answers page 46

2. To say 'I'm not here.'
   - Ⓐ No estoy.
   - Ⓑ No soy.
   - Ⓒ No soy yo.

3. To say 'Is Pedro there?'
   - Ⓐ ¿Es Pedro aquí?
   - Ⓑ ¿Estás Pedro?
   - Ⓒ ¿Está Pedro?

4. To say 'Is that you, Pedro?'
   - Ⓐ ¿Está Pedro?
   - Ⓑ ¿Estás Pedro?
   - Ⓒ ¿Eres Pedro?

5. Complete this exchange with the correct pair of verbs:
   ¿Quién ... ? / ... Pedro.
   - Ⓐ eres / soy
   - Ⓑ estás / soy
   - Ⓒ eres / estoy
   - Ⓓ estás /estoy

6. Complete this exchange with the correct pair of verbs:
   ¿Dónde ... ? / ... aquí.
   - Ⓐ estás / estoy
   - Ⓑ estás / soy
   - Ⓒ eres / soy
   - Ⓓ eres / estoy

7. Select the correct sentence.
   - Ⓐ Soy en casa.
   - Ⓑ Estoy en casa.
   - Ⓒ Soy con un amigo.
   - Ⓓ Estoy el marido de Ana.
   - Ⓔ Estoy Juan.

Tema   **The progressive tense**

The progressive tense (i.e. to be + -ing verb) describes an action in progress.
Select the corresponding progressive form for each sentence.

Answers page 46

1. ¿Qué comes?
   - Ⓐ ¿Qué eres comiendo?
   - Ⓒ ¿Qué estás comando?
   - Ⓑ ¿Qué estás comiendo?
   - Ⓓ ¿Qué eres comiando?

2. ¿Qué hace usted, señora?
   - Ⓐ ¿Qué es hacienda usted, señora?
   - Ⓑ ¿Qué es haciendo usted, señora?
   - Ⓒ ¿Qué está hacienda usted, señora?
   - Ⓓ ¿Qué está haciendo usted, señora?

3. ¿Con quién hablan?
   - Ⓐ ¿Con quién están hablando?
   - Ⓒ ¿Con quién están hablandos?
   - Ⓑ ¿Con quién son hablandos?
   - Ⓓ ¿Con quién son habliendo?

4. Estudio español.
   - Ⓐ Soy estudiando español.
   - Ⓒ Estoy estudiando español.
   - Ⓑ Estoy estudiendo español.
   - Ⓓ Soy estudiendo español.

5. ¿En qué pensáis?
   - Ⓐ ¿En qué sois pensandos?
   - Ⓒ ¿En qué estáis pensando?
   - Ⓑ ¿En qué estáis pensandos?
   - Ⓓ ¿En qué estáis piensendo?

Tema   *Por* and *para*

*Complete each sentence with either **por** or **para**.*

Answers page 46

1. Perdón, ¿puede repetir, ... favor?
   - Ⓐ por
   - Ⓑ para

2. Gracias ... todo, es usted muy amable.
   - Ⓐ por
   - Ⓑ para

3. No hay de qué, estamos aquí ... servirle.

A por   B para

4. ¿... dónde pasas ... ir a a casa ?

A Por / por   B Para / para   C Por / para   D Para / por

Tema **Conjugation: *decir* and *poner***

Choose the correct form of the verb to complete each sentence.

Answers
page 46

1. Un momento, le ... con el señor Sánchez.

A pono   B ponio   C pongo   D poneo

2. ¿Me ... usted su apellido?

A digo   B dice   C dices   D dingo

3. ¿Me ... un poco de música, cariño?

A puenes   B ponges   C pone   D pones

4. ¿Me ... tu número de teléfono?

A dices   B dice   C dece   D deces

5. ¿Sabes mi dirección o te la ...?

A dico   B digo   C deco   D dego

Tema **Spelling and vocabulary**

Select the correctly spelled translation in each case.

1. Can you (formal sing.) repeat your number, please?

A ¿Puede repeter su número, por favor?

Answers
page 46

B ¿Puede repetir su número, por favor?

C ¿Puede repetar su número, por favor?

2. Thank you for your (formal. sing.) patience.

A Gracias por su paciencia.   C Gracias por su pacientia.

B Gracias por su patiencia.

3. You (informal sing.) have a call.

  (A) Tienes una llamada.   (C) Tienes una llamata.

  (B) Tienes una lamada.

4. Can you (informal sing.) call later?

  (A) ¿Puedes llamar más tarde?   (C) ¿Puedes llamar más tardi?

  (B) ¿Puedes llamar más tardo?

Tema   Phone conversations

Choose the most logical order of the phrases in each conversation.

1.

  A.   Hola, ¿puedo hablar con Laura?   (A) A – B – C

  B.   Lo siento, no está.   (B) C – A – B

  C.   Buenos días, ¿en qué puedo ayudarle?   (C) B – A – C

  Answers page 46

2.

  A.   Un momento, por favor, ahora se pone.   (A) C – B – A

  B.   Buenas, ¿me puede poner con Laura?   (B) B – C – A

  C.   Sí, dígame.   (C) A – C – B

3.

  A.   No, lo siento.   (A) C – B – F – A – D – E

  B.   Perdón, ¿con quién quiere usted hablar?   (B) F – B – C – A – E – D

  C.   Hola, cariño, ¿qué tal?   (C) B – D – A – E – F – C

  D.   Oh, disculpe.

  E.   De nada, adiós.

  F.   ¿No eres tú, Antonio?

Unit 5
ÚTILES

Verbs

colgar	*to hang (up)* **Note:** verb with a spelling change: **cuelgo, cuelgas, cuelga, colgamos, colgáis, cuelgan**
comer	*to eat*
decir	*to say, to tell*
poner	*to put* **Note:** on the phone, **poner con** means *to put someone through*: **Te pongo con...** *I'll put you through...*
repetir	*to repeat*
saber	*to know (a fact or how to do something)*

Saying goodbye

adiós	*goodbye*
hasta luego	*see you later*
hasta pronto	*see you soon*
hasta la vista	*see you next time*
hasta mañana	*see you tomorrow*

Addresses

la dirección	*address*
la carretera	*road*
la calle	*street*
la avenida	*avenue*
el paseo	*promenade, public walkway*
la plaza	*town square*

Talking on the phone

el teléfono	*telephone*
llamar por teléfono	*to call on the phone*
el número	*number*
la compañía	*company, firm*
Diga / Dígame	*Hello* (on the phone) Note: These are formal, used in polite or official contexts. In more informal situations, use **Dime**.
No cuelgue / No cuelgues	*Please hold* (formal/informal)
Quisiera hablar con...	*I would like to speak to ...*
Un momento, por favor.	*One moment, please.*
¿Puede / puedes repetir?	*Can you repeat that?* (formal/informal)
¿Puede / puedes llamar más tarde?	*Can you call back later?* (formal/informal)
¿Está Pedro?	*Is Pedro there?*
No, no está.	*No, he's not here.*

Numbers from 100 to 1000

Cien becomes **ciento** between 101 and 199: 101 **ciento uno**; 102 **ciento dos** etc. to 199 **ciento noventa y nueve**. Note that from 200 up, the hundreds must agree with the gender of the noun the number is used with (masculine or feminine).

100	**cien**	600	**seiscientos/as**
200	**doscientos/as**	700	**setecientos/as**
300	**trescientos/as**	800	**ochocientos/as**
400	**cuatrocientos/as**	900	**novecientos/as**
500	**quinientos/as**	1000	**mil**

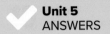

Unit 5
ANSWERS

ESENCIALES

PAGE 38
Some vocabulary
1 **C** 2 **B** 3 **D** 4 **D**

PAGE 38
Addresses
1 **B** 2 **A** 3 **A** 4 **C**

PAGE 39
Telephone numbers
1 **B** 2 **A** 3 **B** 4 **A**

Talking on the phone
1 **C** 2 **A** 3 **B** 4 **A** 5 **B**

PAGE 40
Ser and *estar*
1 **B** 2 **A** 3 **C** 4 **C** 5 **A** 6 **A** 7 **B**

PAGE 41
The progressive tense
1 **B** 2 **D** 3 **A** 4 **C** 5 **C**

Por and *para*
1 **A** 2 **A** 3 **B** 4 **C**

PAGE 42
Decir and *poner*
1 **C** 2 **B** 3 **D** 4 **A** 5 **B**

Spelling and vocabulary
1 **B** 2 **A** 3 **A** 4 **A**

PAGE 43
Phone conversations
1 **B** 2 **A** 3 **A**

YOUR
SCORE:

Did you get between 0 and 8? ¡Ay, ay, ay!

Did you get between 9 and 17? Muy justito...

Did you get between 18 and 26? No está mal, pero...

Did you get between 27 and 35? Enhorabuena.

Did you get 36 or over? ¡Eres un auténtico fenómeno!

| **Tema** | **Giving the time** |

Select the time expressed in each case.

1. Son las cuatro menos veinte de la tarde.
   - (A) 4:20 a.m.
   - (C) 4:20 p.m.
   - (B) 3:40 p.m.

   Answers page 57

2. Son las diez y cinco de la mañana.
   - (A) 10:05 a.m.
   - (C) 5:10 a.m.
   - (B) 10:05 p.m.

3. Son las once y diez de la noche.
   - (A) 10:11 p.m.
   - (C) 11:10 a.m.
   - (B) 11:10 p.m.

4. It is 6:30.
   - (A) Es la seis y media.
   - (C) Son las seis y media.
   - (B) Es las seis y media.

5. It is 10:45.
   - (A) Son las diez y cuarto.
   - (C) Son las once menos cuarto.
   - (B) Es las diez menos cuarto.

6. It is 9:15.
   - (A) Son las nueve y cuarto.
   - (C) Son las nueve menos cuarto.
   - (B) Es las nueve menos cuarto.

7. It is 12:00 midnight.
   - (A) Es la una de la mañana.
   - (C) Son las doce de la noche.
   - (B) Es la una de la noche.

8. It is 12:10.
   - (A) Son las doce y diez.
   - (C) Es medianoche y diez.
   - (B) Es mediodía y diez.

Unit 6
ESENCIALES

Tema **Talking about daily routines**

Which is the most suitable reply in each case?

Answers page 57

1. Te levantas a las cinco de la mañana.
   - A ¡Qué tarde!
   - B ¡Qué temprano!

2. Nos acostamos a la dos de la mañana.
   - A ¡Qué tarde!
   - B ¡Qué temprano!

3. Duerme la siesta a la una de la tarde.
   - A ¡Qué tarde!
   - B ¡Qué temprano!

4. Volvéis del trabajo a las doce de la noche.
   - A ¡Qué tarde!
   - B ¡Qué temprano!

5. Se despiertan a las doce del mediodía.
   - A ¡Qué tarde!
   - B ¡Qué temprano!

6. Salgo del instituto a las siete y media de la tarde.
   - A ¡Qué tarde!
   - B ¡Qué temprano!

Tema **Days of the week**

In each sentence, the days of the week are missing some letters. Choose the answer that completes them.

Answers page 57

1. Los ...les hago deporte.
   - A miérco...
   - B lu...
   - C jue...

2. Salen de copas los ...dos.
   - A mar...
   - B domin...
   - C sába...

3. ¿Nos vemos el mar...?
   - A ...nes
   - B ...tes
   - C ...des

4. ¿Quieres ir al cine el ...ves o el vier...?
   - A lu... / ...tes
   - B miérco... / ...nes
   - C jue... /...nes

5. Ve series en la tele los domin... y los ...nes.
   - A ...gos / lu...
   - B ...dos /jue...
   - C ...dos /vier...

Tema **Prepositions of time**

Complete the sentences with the appropriate preposition of time.

Answers
page 57

1. Los españoles salen mucho ... la noche.
   - Ⓐ a
   - Ⓑ de
   - Ⓒ por

2. Los ingleses comen ... mediodía.
   - Ⓐ a
   - Ⓑ en
   - Ⓒ por

3. ¿... qué hora coméis?
   - Ⓐ A
   - Ⓑ De
   - Ⓒ En

4. Los sábados vuelvo a casa ... madrugada.
   - Ⓐ a
   - Ⓑ de
   - Ⓒ en

5. ... la mañana tengo sueño.
   - Ⓐ En
   - Ⓑ De
   - Ⓒ Por

6. Me levanto temprano, ... las ocho.
   - Ⓐ durante
   - Ⓑ después de
   - Ⓒ antes de

7. Tomo mucho café ... día.
   - Ⓐ durante el
   - Ⓑ después del
   - Ⓒ antes del

8. Te acuestas tarde, ... las once.
   - Ⓐ durante
   - Ⓑ después de
   - Ⓒ antes de

Tema **Prepositions of place**

Complete the sentences with the appropriate preposition(s) of place.

Answers
page 57

1. Los fines de semana me quedo ... casa.
   - Ⓐ a
   - Ⓑ en
   - Ⓒ a la

2. ¿A qué hora sales ... trabajo?
   - Ⓐ del
   - Ⓑ al
   - Ⓒ en

3. Los viernes vuelvo ... casa muy cansado.
   - Ⓐ a la
   - Ⓑ a
   - Ⓒ en

4. ¿Dónde estás, ... casa?

   Ⓐ a 　　　Ⓑ a la 　　　Ⓒ en

5. ¿Vamos ... casa?

   Ⓐ a 　　　Ⓑ en 　　　Ⓒ en la

6. Cuando vuelvo ... trabajo estoy muy cansada.

   Ⓐ de 　　　Ⓑ del 　　　Ⓒ al

7. Trabajo ... España, ... Sevilla.

   Ⓐ a / a 　　　Ⓑ en / en 　　　Ⓒ en / a

8. Vivo ... París, pero nací ... Madrid y vuelvo ... España todos los años.

   Ⓐ a / a / en 　　　Ⓑ en / en / a 　　　Ⓒ en / a / en

Tema	**The verb *soler* (to usually do something)**

Select the corresponding way to say something is usually done in each case.

1. Comes a las dos.

   Ⓐ Sueles comer a las dos.

   Ⓑ Soles comer a las dos.

   Ⓒ Sueles de comer a las dos.

   Answers page 57

2. Salgo de copas los fines de semana.

   Ⓐ Suelo saler de copas los fines de semana.

   Ⓑ Suelo salir de copas los fines de semana.

   Ⓒ Solo de salir de copas los fines de semana.

3. ¿A qué hora os acostáis?

   Ⓐ ¿A qué hora soláis de acostaros?

   Ⓑ ¿A qué hora soléis acostaros?

   Ⓒ ¿A qué hora soléis os acostar?

4. Los sábados me quedo en casa.

   (A) Los sábados suelo me quedar en casa.

   (B) Los sábados solo de me quedar en casa.

   (C) Los sábados suelo quedarme en casa.

5. ¿Cuántas horas duerme usted?

   (A) ¿Cuántas horas sole usted dormir?

   (B) ¿Cuántas horas suele usted dormir?

   (C) ¿Cuántas horas sole usted de dormir?

6. Los españoles toman mucho café.

   (A) Los españoles suelen tomar mucho café.

   (B) Los españoles suelen de tomar mucho café.

   (C) Los españoles solen tomar mucho café.

Tema   This and that

Select the correct form of demonstrative adjective for each sentence.

Answers page 57

1. Estoy muy cansado ... días.

   (A) estas   (B) estos   (C) estes

2. ¿Dónde están ... nuevos bares?

   (A) esas   (B) esos   (C) eses

3. Lo siento, ... semana no puedo verte.

   (A) esta   (B) esto   (C) este

4. No entiendo ... pregunta.

   (A) esa   (B) eso   (C) ese

5. ... fin de semana no voy a salir.

   (A) Esto   (B) Esta   (C) Este

6. ... series son estupendas.

   A Estos   B Estas   C Esto

7. ¿Quién es ... hombre?

   A eso   B esa   C ese

8. ... chicas son estadounidenses.

   A Esos   B Esas   C Eses

Tema **Why? Because ...**

Choose the correct term for each case.

Answers page 57

1. ¿... tienes sueño?

   A Porque   B Por qué

2. Estoy cansado ... duermo poco.

   A porque   B por qué

3. Dime ... te acuestas tan tarde.

   A porque   B por qué

4. No sé ... me preguntas eso.

   A porque   B por qué

5. ¿Piensas que llevo una vida loca ... me acuesto tarde?

   A porque   B por qué

6. No te entiendo: ¿... dices eso?

   A porque   B por qué

Focus **Question words**

Choose the appropriate term in the correct form for each question.

1. ¿... series ves a la semana?

   A Cuántas   C Cuánto

   B Cuándo   D Cuántos

Answers page 57

2. ¿... hora te levantas?

   Ⓐ Cuántas   Ⓒ Cuánta

   Ⓑ Cuándo   Ⓓ A qué

3. ¿... te acuestas?

   Ⓐ Cuánto   Ⓒ Cuánta

   Ⓑ Cuándo   Ⓓ Qué

4. ¿... te pasa?

   Ⓐ Cuánta   Ⓒ Qué

   Ⓑ Cuánto   Ⓓ A qué

5. ¿... bar vamos?

   Ⓐ Cuánto   Ⓒ Qué

   Ⓑ Cuándo   Ⓓ A qué

Tema   **Review: conjugations**

In each sentence, complete the verb with the correct ending or stem.

1. Estáis cansados porque dorm... muy poco.

   Ⓐ ...áis   Ⓑ ...éis   Ⓒ ...ís

                                           Answers page 57

2. Sal... de copas todos los fines de semana.

   Ⓐ ...amos   Ⓑ ...imos   Ⓒ ...emos

3. No quiero salir contigo, ¿me entiend...?

   Ⓐ ...es   Ⓑ ...as   Ⓒ ...is

4. Tengo mucho sueño porque me ...o muy temprano.

   Ⓐ despert...   Ⓑ despiert...   Ⓒ despuert...

5. Los españoles se ...an tarde.

   Ⓐ acuest...   Ⓑ acost...   Ⓒ aciest...

6. ¿A qué hora ...e usted del trabajo?

   Ⓐ vielv...   Ⓑ volv...   Ⓒ vuelv...

Unit 6
ÚTILES

Verbs

acostarse	*to go to bed* Note: verb with a spelling change
despertarse	*to wake up* Note: verb with a spelling change
dormir	*to sleep* Note: verb with a spelling change
entender	*to understand* Note: verb with a spelling change
levantarse	*to get up*
llevar	*to take, to wear, to lead*
pasar	*to pass by* (**Paso por aquí.** *I pass by here.*), *to happen, to occur* (**¿Qué pasa?** *What's happening?* **¿Qué te pasa?** *What happened to you?*)
preguntar	*to ask*
quedarse	*to stay*
salir	*to leave* Note: **ir** (or **salir**) **de copas** *to go out for a drink*
soler	*to usually do something* Note: verb with a spelling change
tomar	*to take, to have* (eat or drink)
volver	*to return* Note: verb with a spelling change

Talking about time

la hora	*hour, time*
el minuto	*minute*
¿Qué hora es?	*What time is it?*
Es la una.	*It's 1:00.*
Son las dos, son las tres...	*It's 2:00, it's 3:00,* etc.
en punto	*on the dot*
y media	*half past*
y cuarto	*quarter past*

menos cuarto	*a quarter to* Note: this literally means 'minus quarter'. If the context isn't obvious, you can indicate the time of day: **de la mañana** *in the morning;* **de la tarde** *in the afternoon;* **de la noche** *at night.*

Days of the week

lunes	*Monday*
martes	*Tuesday*
miércoles	*Wednesday*
jueves	*Thursday*
viernes	*Friday*
sábado	*Saturday*
domingo	*Sunday*
la semana	*week*
el fin de semana	*weekend*

Saying when

antes	*before*
después	*after* Note: 'before' and 'after' are often used with the preposition **de** in Spanish: **antes de / después de: después del trabajo** *after work.*
durante	*during*
de día, de noche	*by day, by night*
por la mañana, por la tarde, por la noche	*in the morning, in the afternoon, in the evening/at night*
a mediodía	*at midday, at noon*
de madrugada	*in the early morning, at daybreak*
temprano	*early*
tarde	*late*

Unit 6
ÚTILES

Asking and responding to questions

¿cuándo?	*When?*
¿por qué?	*Why?*
porque	*because*

Nouns

el amigo, la amiga	*friend* (m./f.)
el bar	*bar*
el cine	*cinema, movie theatre*
el sueño	*sleep, dream*
la serie	*TV series*
la siesta	*nap*
la tele	*television*
la vida	*life*

Adjectives and demonstratives

cansado/a	*tired* (m./f.)
estupendo/a	*amazing* (m./f.)
loco/a	*crazy* (m./f.)
este hombre, estos hombres	*this man, these men*
esta mujer, estas mujeres	*this woman, these women*
ese hombre, esos hombres	*that man, those men*
esa mujer, esas mujeres	*that woman, those women*
esto	*this one*
eso	*that one*

ESENCIALES

PAGE 47
Giving the time
1 **B** 2 **A** 3 **B** 4 **C** 5 **C** 6 **A** 7 **C** 8 **A**

PAGE 48
Talking about daily routines
1 **B** 2 **A** 3 **B** 4 **A** 5 **A** 6 **A**

Days of the week
1 **A** 2 **C** 3 **B** 4 **C** 5 **A**

PAGE 49
Prepositions of time
1 **C** 2 **A** 3 **A** 4 **B** 5 **C** 6 **C** 7 **A** 8 **B**

Prepositions of place
1 **B** 2 **A** 3 **B** 4 **C** 5 **A** 6 **B** 7 **B** 8 **B**

PAGE 50
The verb *soler* (to usually do something)
1 **A** 2 **B** 3 **B** 4 **C** 5 **B** 6 **A**

PAGE 51
This and that
1 **B** 2 **B** 3 **A** 4 **A** 5 **C** 6 **B** 7 **C** 8 **B**

PAGE 52
Why? Because ...
1 **B** 2 **A** 3 **B** 4 **B** 5 **A** 6 **B**

Question words
1 **A** 2 **D** 3 **B** 4 **C** 5 **D**

PAGE 53
Conjugations
1 **C** 2 **B** 3 **A** 4 **B** 5 **A** 6 **C**

YOUR SCORE:

Did you get between 0 and 12? ¡Ay, ay, ay!

Did you get between 13 and 25? Muy justito...

Did you get between 26 and 38? No está mal, pero...

Did you get between 39 and 51? Enhorabuena.

Did you get 52 or over? ¡Eres un auténtico fenómeno!

Unit 7
ESENCIALES

Tema **Family**

Choose which family member is described.

Answers page 68

1. La madre de mi madre es...
   - (A) mi tía.
   - (B) mi abuela.
   - (C) mi nieta.

2. El hermano de mi padre es...
   - (A) mi tío.
   - (B) mi abuelo.
   - (C) mi primo.

3. El hijo de mi hermana es...
   - (A) mi primo.
   - (B) mi sobrino.
   - (C) mi nieto.

4. La hija de mi tío es...
   - (A) mi nieta.
   - (B) mi sobrina.
   - (C) mi prima.

5. El hijo de mi hija es...
   - (A) mi nieto.
   - (B) mi sobrino.
   - (C) mi primo.

Tema **At the table**

Complete the missing letters in these words to do with dining.

Answers page 68

1. Es hora de comer, pongo la me...
   - (A) ...la.
   - (B) ...ta.
   - (C) ...sa.

2. Para beber, me sirvo de un va...
   - (A) ...ro.
   - (B) ...so.
   - (C) ...to.

3. ¿Pongo cucha... o no?
   - (A) ...tas
   - (B) ...ras
   - (C) ...llas

4. ¿Cuántos pla... pongo?
   - (A) ...tos
   - (B) ...tas
   - (C) ...tes

5. ¿Cuántos cubier... pongo?
   - (A) ...tos
   - (B) ...tas
   - (C) ...tes

6. Para comer carne, me sirvo de un cuchi... y de un tene...

   (A) ...llo / ...dor.　　(B) ...to / ...dora.　　(C) ...ro / ...tor.

7. ¿Dónde están las servi... y el man...?

   (A) ...ettas / ...tón　　(B) ...etas / ...to　　(C) ...lletas / ...tel

Tema　Meals and food

Select the missing words that are in the right order to complete each sentence.

1. Mi ..... es un ..... con ..... y ..... de ......

   (A) café / leche / desayuno / mantequilla / tostadas

   (B) desayuno / café / leche / tostadas / mantequilla

   (C) mantequilla / café / tostadas / leche / desayuno

   Answers page 68

2. De ..... voy a tomar un ....., de ..... una ..... y de ..... un ......

   (A) gazpacho / primero / postre / tortilla / flan / segundo

   (B) postre / primero / gazpacho / segundo / tortilla /flan

   (C) primero / gazpacho / segundo / tortilla / postre / flan

3. Tengo .....: voy a ..... un ..... con ......

   (A) churros / merendar / chocolate / hambre

   (B) merendar / hambre / churros / chocolate

   (C) hambre / merendar / chocolate / churros

4. Mis ..... suelen ser una ..... con .... en la ......

   (A) cenas / hamburguesa / patatas / fritas / cocina

   (B) patatas / cocina / cenas / fritas / hamburguesa

   (C) fritas / cocina / patatas / hamburguesa / cenas

Unit 7
ESENCIALES

Tema **Negative sentences**

Choose the most suitable negative word for each context.

1. Cuando mi madre hace tortilla, no dejo ... en el plato.
   - A nada
   - B nadie
   - C nunca
   - D tampoco

   Answers page 68

2. En casa pongo la mesa pero no lavo ... los platos.
   - A nada
   - B nadie
   - C nunca
   - D tampoco

3. No tienes hambre y yo ...
   - A nada.
   - B nadie.
   - C nunca.
   - D tampoco.

4. Los fines de semana no veo a ...
   - A nada.
   - B nadie.
   - C nunca.
   - D tampoco.

Tema **Personal pronouns**

Select the correct form of these personal pronouns used with prepositions.

1. No puedo vivir ...
   - A sin ti.
   - B sintigo.
   - C sin te.

   Answers page 68

2. ¿Quieres cenar...
   - A con yo?
   - B con mí?
   - C conmigo?

3. Muchas gracias...
   - A a vosotros.
   - B a os.
   - C a vuestro.

4. La familia es importante...
   - A para sus.
   - B para les.
   - C para ellos.

5. Esto lo hago...

   Ⓐ por le.   Ⓑ por su.   Ⓒ por usted.

6. No quiero salir...

   Ⓐ con te.   Ⓑ contigo.   Ⓒ con ti.

7. ¿Qué dice...

   Ⓐ de me?   Ⓑ de mí?   Ⓒ de yo?

Tema   Antonyms

Identify the opposite of each of these sentences.

Answers page 68

1. Estoy sentado.

   Ⓐ Estoy de pie.   Ⓒ Estoy loco.

   Ⓑ Estoy durmiendo.

2. Estamos equivocados.

   Ⓐ Estamos juntos.   Ⓒ Tenemos razón.

   Ⓑ Estamos de acuerdo.

3. Mi primo siempre lava los platos.

   Ⓐ Mi primo también lava los platos.   Ⓒ Mi primo nunca lava los platos.

   Ⓑ Mi primo tampoco lava los platos.

4. Está cansada.

   Ⓐ Está fenomenal.   Ⓒ Tiene sueño.

   Ⓑ Tiene hambre.

5. Los niños meriendan ahora.

   Ⓐ Los niños meriendan así.   Ⓒ Los niños meriendan después.

   Ⓑ Los niños meriendan solos.

Unit 7
ESENCIALES

Answers page 68

| **Tema** | **The impersonal subject 'one'** |

For each sentence, choose the equivalent that is expressed using an impersonal subject ('one').

1. Hoy escribimos menos cartas.

   A Hoy se escribe menos cartas.

   B Hoy se escriben menos cartas.

2. En casa cenamos a las diez.

   A En casa se cena a las diez.

   B En casa se cenan a las diez.

3. En mi familia comemos muchas patatas.

   A En mi familia se come muchas patatas.

   B En mi familia se comen muchas patatas.

4. No siempre tenemos razón.

   A No siempre se tiene razón.

   B No siempre se tienen razón.

5. Cuando estamos de mal humor, decimos cosas que no pensamos.

   A Cuando se están de mal humor, se dicen cosas que no se piensan.

   B Cuando se está de mal humor, se dicen cosas que no se piensan.

   C Cuando se están de mal humor, se dicen cosas que no se piensa.

   D Cuando se está de mal humor, se dice cosas que no se piensan.

| **Tema** | **Conjugation: *sentir* and *sentar*** |

Choose the correct verb for each context.

Answers page 68

1. ¿Te ... bien o llamo a un médico?

   A sientas   B sientes

2. Lo ..., no podemos salir de copas.

   A sentamos   B sentimos

3. ¿Por qué no os ... para cenar?

    (A) sentáis   (B) sentís

4. El profesor entra y se ...

    (A) sienta.   (B) siente.

5. Los niños ... cariño por lo animales.

    (A) sientan   (B) sienten

| **Tema** | **Very, much, a lot** |

Select the correct translation for each sentence.

**Answers
page 68**

1. My sister doesn't eat much.

    (A) Mi hermana no come muy.

    (B) Mi hermana no come mucho.

    (C) Mi hermana no come mucha.

2. I eat a lot of hamburgers.

    (A) Como muy hamburguesas.

    (B) Como muchos hamburguesas.

    (C) Como muchas hamburguesas.

3. They don't wash many plates.

    (A) No lavan muy platos.

    (B) No lavan muchos platos.

    (C) No lavan muchas platos.

4. Family is very important.

    (A) La familia es muy importante.

    (B) La familia es mucho importante.

    (C) La familia es mucha importante.

Unit 7
ESENCIALES

5. I'm very sleepy.

- Ⓐ Tengo muy sueño.

- Ⓑ Tengo mucho sueño.

- Ⓒ Tengo mucha sueño.

Tema **Masculine and feminine: exceptions**

All of these nouns are feminine in Spanish. But not all of them take the article you might expect. Choose the option with the correct article.

1. Eagle
   - Ⓐ El águila
   - Ⓑ La águila

Answers page 68

2. Classroom
   - Ⓐ El aula
   - Ⓑ La aula

3. Anchovy
   - Ⓐ El anchoa
   - Ⓑ La anchoa

4. Hunger
   - Ⓐ El hambre
   - Ⓑ La hambre

5. Pavement, sidewalk
   - Ⓐ El acera
   - Ⓑ La acera

6. Hammock
   - Ⓐ El hamaca
   - Ⓑ La hamaca

7. Dear friend
   - Ⓐ La amiga querida
   - Ⓒ El amiga querido
   - Ⓑ El amiga querida

8. White flour
   - Ⓐ La harina blanca
   - Ⓒ El harina blanco
   - Ⓑ El harina blanca

9. Cool water
    A La agua fresca
    C El agua fresco
    B El agua fresca

10. I'm very hungry.
    A Tengo mucha hambre.
    B Tengo mucho hambre.

Verbs

ÚTILES

beber	to drink
cenar	to dine
dejar	to leave, to let (allow)
desayunar	to eat breakfast
escribir	to write
lavar	to wash
merendar	to snack Note: verb with a spelling change
sentir	to feel, to be sorry Note: verb with a spelling change
sentarse	to sit down Note: verb with a spelling change

Meals

el desayuno	breakfast
la comida	food, meal, lunch Note: in some regions, **el almuerzo** is used to refer to either lunch or a mid-morning snack.
la merienda	afternoon snack
la cena	dinner
el primero	starter, first course
el segundo	main course
el postre	dessert

Unit 7
ÚTILES

Table settings

la mesa	table
el mantel	tablecloth
la servilleta	serviette, napkin
los cubiertos	cutlery
el cuchillo	knife
el plato	plate
el tenedor	fork
el vaso	glass
la cuchara	spoon

Family

la familia	family
el padre	father Note: **los padres** refers to parents.
papá	dad
la madre	mother
mamá	mum, mom
el abuelo / la abuela	grandfather / grandmother Note: **los abuelos** refers to grandparents.
el hermano / la hermana	brother / sister
el tío / la tía	uncle / aunt
el primo / la prima	cousin (m./f.)
el sobrino / la sobrina	nephew / niece
el nieto / la nieta	grandson / granddaughter

A few foods

la carne	*meat*
la tostada	*toast*
la mantequilla	*butter*
la tortilla	*Spanish omelette*
el flan	*crème caramel*
la hamburguesa	*hamburger*
la patata	*potato* Note: the term for *fries* is **patatas fritas**.

Useful expressions

tener hambre	*to be hungry*
tener razón	*to be right*
estar equivocado	*to be wrong*

Negative words

nada	*nothing*
nadie	*no one*
nunca	*never*
tampoco	*neither, nor*

Adverbs and adverbial expressions

ahora	*now*
así	*like this/that, thus*
de pie	*on foot, standing up*
hoy	*today*
juntos	*together*
siempre	*always*

67

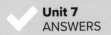

ESENCIALES

PAGE 58
Family
1 **B** 2 **A** 3 **B** 4 **C** 5 **A**

At the table
1 **C** 2 **B** 3 **B** 4 **A** 5 **A** 6 **A** 7 **C**

PAGE 59
Meals and food
1 **B** 2 **C** 3 **C** 4 **A**

PAGE 60
Negative sentences
1 **A** 2 **C** 3 **D** 4 **B**

Personal pronouns
1 **A** 2 **C** 3 **A** 4 **C** 5 **C** 6 **B** 7 **B**

PAGE 61
Antonyms
1 **A** 2 **C** 3 **C** 4 **A** 5 **C**

PAGE 62
The impersonal subject 'one'
1 **B** 2 **A** 3 **B** 4 **A** 5 **B**

Conjugations: *sentir* and *sentar*
1 **B** 2 **B** 3 **A** 4 **A** 5 **B**

PAGE 63
Very, much, a lot
1 **B** 2 **C** 3 **B** 4 **A** 5 **B**

PAGE 64
Masculine and feminine: some exceptions
1 **A** 2 **A** 3 **B** 4 **A** 5 **B** 6 **B** 7 **A** 8 **A** 9 **B** 10 **A**

YOUR SCORE:

Did you get between 0 and 10? ¡Ay, ay, ay!

Did you get between 11 and 21? Muy justito...

Did you get between 22 and 32? No está mal, pero...

Did you get between 33 and 43? Enhorabuena.

Did you get 44 or over? ¡Eres un auténtico fenómeno!

| **Tema** | **Numbers from 1000** |

Select the number written out in words that corresponds to each figure.

1. Un día tiene 1440 minutos.

   Ⓐ mil cuatrocientos cuarenta

   Ⓑ mil cuatrocientas cuarenta

   Ⓒ mil ciento cuarenta

2. El volcán Teide tiene una altitud de 3 718 metros.

   Ⓐ trece mil setenta y ocho

   Ⓑ trece mil sietecientos dieciocho

   Ⓒ tres mil setecientos dieciocho

3. Tengo 12 562 amigas de Facebook.

   Ⓐ dos mil cinco ciento setenta y dos

   Ⓑ doce mil quinientas sesenta y dos

   Ⓒ diez mil cincuenta sesenta y dos

4. El Nou Camp tiene capacidad para 99 354 personas.

   Ⓐ noventa y nueve mil trescientos cincuenta y cuatro

   Ⓑ novecientos noventa y tres mil cincuenta y cuatro

   Ⓒ noventa y nueve mil trescientas cincuenta y cuatro

5. El Fútbol Club Barcelona tiene 143 855 socios.

   Ⓐ ciento cuarenta y tres mil ochocientos cincuenta y cinco

   Ⓑ catorce y tres mil ochocientos cincuenta y cinco

   Ⓒ cien mil cuarenta y tres mil ochocientos cincuenta y cinco

6. Madrid tiene 3 265 038 habitantes.

   Ⓐ tres millones doscientos seis mil quinientos treinta y ocho

   Ⓑ tres millones doscientos sesenta y cinco mil treinta y ocho

   Ⓒ trece millones veintiséis mil quinientos treinta y ocho

7. España tiene 46 659 302 habitantes.

   A cuatro millones sesenta y seis mil cincuenta y nueve mil trescientos dos

   B sesenta y cuatro millones sesenta y cinco nueve mil treinta y dos

   C cuarenta y seis millones seiscientos cincuenta y nueve mil trescientos dos

8. 23 777 015 son mujeres.

   A veintitrés millones setecientos setento y siete mil quince

   B veintitrés millones setecientas setenta y siete mil quince

   C veintitrés millones setecientos setenta y siete mil quince

Tema   Around the home: rooms and furnishings

Choose the furniture or appliance you might expect to find in each room.

1. la cocina

   A el váter   B el horno

   Answers page 79

2. el dormitorio

   A la mesa   B la cama

3. el salón

   A el sillón   B el frigorífico

4. el comedor

   A la silla   B la lavadora

5. el cuarto de baño

   A el microondas   B la ducha

Tema   Good and bad points

A choosy client is visiting an apartment. He acknowledges its good points, but mainly points out its flaws. Select the correct order of the adjectives.

1. El piso es...

   A caro pero grande.   B grande pero caro.

   Answers page 79

2. El váter es...

   A limpio pero feo.   B feo pero limpio.

3. El salón es...
   - (A) agradable pero pequeño.
   - (B) pequeño pero agradable.

4. El barrio es...
   - (A) un poco sucio pero barato.
   - (B) barato pero un poco sucio.

5. Los muebles son...
   - (A) viejos pero bonitos.
   - (B) bonitos pero viejos.

6. Los vecinos son...
   - (A) amables pero ruidosos.
   - (B) ruidosos pero amables.

7. Los electrodomésticos son...
   - (A) antiguos pero buenos.
   - (B) buenos pero antiguos.

Tema | **Verbs that require an indirect object: *gustar*, *encantar*, etc.**

Choose the pronouns in the right order to complete these sentences.

1. A ... ... gusta España.
   - (A) nos / nosotros
   - (B) nosotros / nos
   - (C) nuestro / nos

2. A ... ... gusta Andalucía.
   - (A) su / ella
   - (B) le / la
   - (C) ella / le

Answers page 79

3. A ... ... gusta salir.
   - (A) vosotros / os
   - (B) os / vosotros
   - (C) vos / os

4. A ... no ... gusta este barrio.
   - (A) me / mi
   - (B) yo / mí
   - (C) mí / me

5. ¿A ... ... gusta Shakira?
   - (A) le / usted
   - (B) usted / le
   - (C) usted / se

6. A ... no ... gusta trabajar.
   - (A) ti / te
   - (B) tú / te
   - (C) te / tu

7. A ... no ... gusta la paella.
   - (A) les / se
   - (B) ellos / ustedes
   - (C) ellos / les

Unit 8
ESENCIALES

For each sentence, choose the correct form of the verb.

Answers page 79

1. Me ... los animales.
   - A gusta
   - B gustan

2. ¿Os ... tener animales en casa?
   - A gusta
   - B gustan

3. Le ... los gatos.
   - A encanta
   - B encantan

4. No nos ... los perros.
   - A encanta
   - B encantan

5. Te ... acostarte tarde.
   - A horroriza
   - B horrorizan

6. Nos ... salir de copas.
   - A horroriza
   - B horrorizan

Tema *Querer* or *gustar*?

In English, we use 'love' to talk about tastes as well as feelings. For each context, choose the most appropriate way to convey the idea in Spanish.

1. ellos ♥ los fines de semana
   - A Les gustan los fines de semana.
   - B Quieren los fines de semana.

2. vosotros ♥ Navidad
   - A Os gusta Navidad.
   - B Queréis Navidad.

Answers page 79

3. tú ♥ tus hermanos
   - A Te gustan tus hermanos.
   - B Quieres a tus hermanos.

4. nosotros ♥ las ciudades pequeñas
   - A Nos gustan las ciudades pequeñas.
   - B Queremos las ciudades pequeñas.

5. yo ♥ mis padres
   - A Me gustan mis padres.
   - B Quiero a mis padres.

6. ella ♥ su abuela

Ⓐ Le gusta su abuela.   Ⓑ Quiere a su abuela.

Tema **Intensifiers and exclamations**

Answers
page 79

Select the corresponding translation for each case.

1. It's a very affordable rent.

   Ⓐ Es un alquiler más barato.

   Ⓑ Es un alquiler muy barato.

   Ⓒ Es un alquiler mucho barato.

2. The bed is very small.

   Ⓐ La cama es pequeñísima.

   Ⓑ La cama es la más pequeña.

   Ⓒ La cama es más pequeña.

3. This bedroom is the nicest.

   Ⓐ Esta habitación es la muy agradable.

   Ⓑ Esta habitación es la más agradable.

   Ⓒ Esta habitación es más agradable.

4. The cockroach is the most unpleasant animal.

   Ⓐ La cucaracha es el animal muy desagradable.

   Ⓑ La cucaracha es el animal el más desagradable.

   Ⓒ La cucaracha es el animal más desagradable.

5. What a large TV!

   Ⓐ ¡Qué tele más grande!

   Ⓑ ¡Qué más grande tele!

   Ⓒ ¡Qué muy grande tele!

6. How ugly those furnishings are!

(A) ¡Qué feos estos muebles son!

(B) ¡Qué feos son estos muebles!

(C) ¡Qué más feos son estos muebles!

Tema Commands

Select if each command is informal or formal.

Answers page 79

1. ¡Lava los platos!
   (A) informal   (B) formal

2. ¡Limpie el váter!
   (A) informal   (B) formal

3. ¡Coma rápido!
   (A) informal   (B) formal

4. ¡Escriba más cartas!
   (A) informal   (B) formal

5. ¡Visita España!
   (A) informal   (B) formal

6. ¡Perdone!
   (A) informal   (B) formal

7. ¡Bebe agua!
   (A) informal   (B) formal

8. ¡Dígame la verdad!
   (A) informal   (B) formal

9. Lo siento, disculpa.
   (A) informal   (B) formal

Tema Conjugations: *venir*, *empezar*, *preferir*

Complete the exchange with the missing question or response.

1. ¿De dónde vienes? / ...

   Ⓐ Venio de casa.　　　Ⓑ Vengo de casa.

   Answers page 79

2. ¿A qué venís? / ...

   Ⓐ Venimos a visitar el piso.　　　Ⓑ Vienimos a visitar el piso.

3. ... / Preferimos los perros.

   Ⓐ ¿Preferéis los perros o los gatos?　　　Ⓑ ¿Preferís los perros o los gatos?

4. ... / Prefiero ir al cine.

   Ⓐ ¿Preferes ver la tele o ir al cine?　　　Ⓑ ¿Prefieres ver la tele o ir al cine?

5. ¿Cuándo empezáis a visitar pisos? / ...

   Ⓐ Empiezamos este jueves.　　　Ⓑ Empezamos este jueves.

6. ... / ¡Empiezo hoy!

   Ⓐ ¿Cuándo empiezas a trabajar?　　　Ⓑ ¿Cuándo empezas a trabajar?

Tema Stepfamilies

Select the relationships between the people in these stepfamilies.
Julia y Andrés están separados. Tienen una hija juntos: Andrea. Julia vive con Carlos, que tiene un hijo de un matrimonio anterior: Daniel. Andrés vive con Ana y tienen un hijo juntos: Nicolás.

1. Carlos es...

   Ⓐ el padre de Andrea.　　　Ⓒ el hermanastro de Andrea.

   Ⓑ el padrastro de Andrea.

   Answers page 79

2. Andrea es...

   Ⓐ la hermanastra de Daniel.　　　Ⓒ la madrastra de Daniel.

   Ⓑ la hermana de Daniel.

Unit 8
ESENCIALES

3. Julia es...

  (A) la madre de Daniel. (C) la hermanastra de Daniel.

  (B) la madrastra de Daniel.

4. Nicolás es...

  (A) el hermano de Andrea. (C) el padrastro de Andrea.

  (B) el hermanastro de Andrea.

Verbs

ÚTILES

disculpar	*to excuse*
empezar	*to start* Note: verb with a spelling change
encantar	*to delight, to enchant*
gustar	*to appeal to, to be pleasing, to like*
lavar	*to wash*
limpiar	*to clean*
preferir	*to prefer* Note: verb with a spelling change
querer	*to like, to love* Note: verb with a spelling change
venir	*to come*
visitar	*to visit*

Large numbers

mil	*thousand*
dos mil	*two thousand*
cien mil	*hundred thousand*
ciento cincuenta mil	*one hundred and fifty thousand*
un millón	*one million*
cien millones	*one hundred million*
mil millones	*one billion*

The home

el alquiler	*rent*
el barrio	*neighbourhood*
la cocina	*kitchen*
el comedor	*dining room*
el dormitorio	*bedroom*
la ducha	*shower*
el cuarto de baño	*bathroom*
la habitación	*room, bedroom*
el piso	*apartment, flat*
el salón	*lounge, living room*

Furniture and appliances

la cama	*bed*
el electrodoméstico	*electrical appliances*
el frigorífico	*refrigerator*
el horno	*oven*
la lavadora	*washing machine*
el microondas	*microwave*
el mueble	*furniture*
la silla	*chair*
el sillón	*armchair*
el váter	*toilet, WC*

Stepfamily

separado/a	*separated* (m./f.)
divorciado/a	*divorced* (m./f.)

la pareja	*couple*
el padrastro	*stepfather*
la madrastra	*stepmother*
el hermanastro / la hermanastra	*stepbrother / stepsister* Note: these terms are used when siblings do not have a parent in common; if they share a mother or father, i.e. are half-brothers or half-sisters, **el hermano, la hermana** are used.

Nouns

el animal	*animal*
el perro	*dog*
el gato	*cat*

Adjectives

agradable	*nice, pleasant*
amable	*kind*
antiguo/a	*old* (m./f.)
barato/a	*cheap, inexpensive* (m./f.)
caro/a	*expensive* (m./f.)
desagradable	*unpleasant*
feo/a	*ugly* (m./f.)
grande	*big, large*
limpio/a	*clean* (m./f.)
pequeño/a	*small* (m./f.)
ruidoso/a	*noisy* (m./f.)
sucio/a	*dirty* (m./f.)
viejo/a	*old* (m./f.)

ESENCIALES

PAGE 69
Numbers from 1000
1 **A** 2 **C** 3 **B** 4 **C** 5 **A** 6 **B** 7 **C** 8 **B**

. . . .

PAGE 70
Around the home: rooms and furnishings
1 **B** 2 **B** 3 **A** 4 **A** 5 **B**

Good and bad points
1 **B** 2 **A** 3 **A** 4 **B** 5 **B** 6 **A** 7 **B**

. . . .

PAGE 71
Verbs that require an indirect object: *gustar*, *encantar*, etc.
1 **B** 2 **C** 3 **A** 4 **C** 5 **B** 6 **A** 7 **C**
1 **B** 2 **A** 3 **B** 4 **B** 5 **A** 6 **A**

. . . .

PAGE 72
Querer or *gustar*?
1 **A** 2 **A** 3 **B** 4 **A** 5 **B** 6 **B**

. . . .

PAGE 73
Intensifiers and exclamations
1 **B** 2 **A** 3 **B** 4 **C** 5 **A** 6 **B**

. . . .

PAGE 74
Commands
1 **A** 2 **B** 3 **B** 4 **B** 5 **A** 6 **B** 7 **A** 8 **B** 9 **A**

. . . .

PAGE 75
Conjugations: *venir*, *empezar*, *preferir*
1 **B** 2 **A** 3 **B** 4 **B** 5 **B** 6 **A**

. . . .

Stepfamilies
1 **B** 2 **A** 3 **B** 4 **A**

YOUR SCORE:

Did you get between 0 and 12? ¡Ay, ay, ay!

Did you get between 13 and 25? Muy justito...

Did you get between 26 and 38? No está mal, pero...

Did you get between 39 and 51? Enhorabuena.

Did you get 52 or over? ¡Eres un auténtico fenómeno!

Unit 9
ESENCIALES

Tema **Describing characteristics**

Select the opposite of each description.

Answers page 89

1. Es baja.
   - Ⓐ Es rubia.
   - Ⓑ Es alta.

2. Son tontos.
   - Ⓐ Son listos.
   - Ⓑ Son morenos.

3. Sois delgados.
   - Ⓐ Sois pelirrojos.
   - Ⓑ Sois gordos.

4. Somos buenas.
   - Ⓐ Somos inteligentes.
   - Ⓑ Somos malas.

Tema **The face**

Choose the most suitable word to complete each sentence.

Answers page 89

1. Tengo las ... pequeñas.
   - Ⓐ dientes
   - Ⓑ ojos
   - Ⓒ orejas

2. Llevas el ... largo.
   - Ⓐ nariz
   - Ⓑ cara
   - Ⓒ pelo

3. Tienen la ... roja.
   - Ⓐ nariz
   - Ⓑ pelo
   - Ⓒ labio

4. Tenéis los ... grandes.
   - Ⓐ dientes
   - Ⓑ bocas
   - Ⓒ caras

5. Tienes los ... verdes.
   - Ⓐ lenguas
   - Ⓑ ojos
   - Ⓒ orejas

6. Tiene los ... pequeños.
   - Ⓐ lenguas
   - Ⓑ labios
   - Ⓒ bocas

Tema   Too much, a lot, quite, enough

Choose the correct form of the word for each context.

Answers page 89

1. Mis vecinos son ... simpáticos.
   - A bastante
   - B bastantes

2. Esta chica es ... antipática.
   - A bastanta
   - B bastante

3. Estamos ... enfadados contigo.
   - A bastante
   - B bastantes

4. No leéis ... libros.
   - A bastante
   - B bastantes

5. ¿Hay ... sillas?
   - A bastante
   - B bastantes
   - C bastantas

6. Mis hermanas están ... bien, gracias.
   - A bastante
   - B bastantes
   - C bastantas

7. Mis amigas ven ... la tele.
   - A demasiado
   - B demasiada
   - C demasiadas

8. Me gustan ... las fiestas.
   - A demasiado
   - B demasiados
   - C demasiadas

9. Estos pisos son ... caros.
   - A demasiado
   - B demasiados
   - C demasiadas

10. Tenéis ... amigas en Facebook.
    - A demasiado
    - B demasiada
    - C demasiadas

11. Tengo tres cumpleaños esta semana: ¡son ...!
    - A demasiado
    - B demasiados
    - C demasiadas

12. Comen ... carne.
    - A demasiado
    - B demasiada
    - C demasiados

Unit 9
ESENCIALES

| **Tema** | **To want to, to feel like** |

*Select the sentence using **apetecer** that conveys the same meaning as the sentence constructed with **tener ganas de**.*

Answers page 89

1. No tengo ganas de ir al cine.

   A No me apetece de ir al cine.

   B No me apetece ir al cine.

   C No me apetezco ir al cine.

2. ¿Tienes ganas de hacer una fiesta de cumpleaños?

   A ¿Te apeteces de hacer una fiesta de cumpleaños?

   B ¿Te apetece hacer una fiesta de cumpleaños?

   C ¿Te apetece de hacer una fiesta de cumpleaños?

3. No tiene usted ganas de fiestas.

   A No le apetecen las fiestas.

   B No se apetece las fiestas.

   C No se apetecen de las fiestas.

4. Tenemos ganas de unos churros.

   A Nos apetece de unos churros.

   B Nos apetecemos unos churros.

   C Nos apetecen unos churros.

5. No tienen ganas de ver a nadie.

   A No les apetecen ver a nadie.

   B No les apetece ver a nadie.

   C No les apetecen de ver a nadie.

6. ¿Tenéis ganas de ir de compras?

   A ¿Os apetecen de ir de compras?

   B ¿Os apetece ir de compras?

   C ¿Os apetecéis ir de compras?

Tema Using the verb *parecer*

Choose the correct translation in each case.

Answers page 89

1. She seems nice.

   A La parezco simpática.

   B Se parezco simpática.

   C Me parece simpática.

2. Do the neighbours seem pleasant?

   A ¿Pareces agradables los vecinos?

   B ¿Te parecen agradables los vecinos?

   C ¿Se pareces agradables los vecinos?

3. I think we know him.

   A Parecemos que lo conocemos.

   B Nos parece que lo conocemos.

   C Nos parecemos que lo conocemos.

4. I resemble my grandfather.

   A Me parezco a mi abuelo.

   B Me parece a mi abuelo.

   C Se parezco a mi abuelo.

5. You look like each other.

   A Vosotros parecéis.

   B Os parecéis.

   C Os parece.

6. You look a lot like me.

   A Me pareces mucho.

   B Te parezco mucho.

   C Te pareces mucho a mí.

Unit 9
ESENCIALES

Answers page 89

Tema The expression *caer bien / mal*, etc.

Choose the correct translation for each sentence.

1. Me caes muy bien.

   A I find you really nice.
   B You find me really nice.

2. Le cae mal a mi madre.

   A My mother doesn't like him.
   B He doesn't like my mother.

3. ¿Cómo te caen?

   A What do they think of you?
   B What do you think of them?

4. Les caigo fatal.

   A I can't stand them.
   B They can't stand me.

5. Creo que os caemos regular.

   A I think that we get along with you okay.
   B I think that you get along with us okay.

6. Nos caen fenomenal.

   A We love them.
   B They love us.

Tema Possessive pronouns and adjectives

Select the correct order of pronouns in each case.

Answers page 89

1. ... cumpleaños es el jueves y ... es el domingo.

   A Mío / el tu
   C Mis / los tuyos
   B Mi / el tuyo

2. ... gafas son negras y ... son marrones.

   A Tus / las sus
   C Tus / las suyas
   B Tu / el suya

3. ... nariz es pequeña y ... es grande.

   A Su / el mío
   C Sus / los míos
   B Su / la mía

84

4. ... amigos son simpáticos y ... son pijos.

  A Nuestros / los vuestros

  C Nos / los vo

  B Nuestros / las vosotras

5. ... casa es amarilla y ... es azul.

  A Os / mía

  C Vuestra / la mía

  B Usted / la mía

Tema *Pero* (but) or *sino* (but rather, not only ... but)?

Select the correct term for each context.

Answers page 89

1. Quiero adelgazar ... no quiero hacer deporte.

  A pero   B sino   C sino que

2. No es rubia ... morena.

  A pero   B sino   C sino que

3. Me gustan los regalos ... no me gustan las fiestas.

  A pero   B sino   C sino que

4. No es solo tonto ... también antipático.

  A pero   B sino   C sino que

5. No solo hablo chino ... también lo escribo.

  A pero   B sino   C sino que

Tema Usage of prepositions

Select the missing preposition in each case.

Answers page 89

1. ¿Crees ... Dios?

  A a   B en   C de

2. No es mala, pero ... mi opinión es demasiado pija.

  A a   B en   C con

3. No es feo, pero ... mi gusto es demasiado bajo.

   A en   B de   C para

4. ¿Estáis seguros ... que no queréis venir?

   A en   B de   C con

5. ¿Estáis enfadados ... serio?

   A a   B de   C en

6. Pienso mucho ... ti.

   A a   B en   C por

Verbs   ÚTILES

adelgazar	*to lose weight*
apetecer	*to feel like*
caer	*to fall* Note: **caer(le) bien/mal** *to like/dislike someone* (conjugates like **gustar**)
conocer	*to know of, to be familiar with*
creer	*to believe* Note: **creer en** *to believe in*
parecer	*to seem*
parecerse	*to resemble, to look like*
regalar	*to offer as a gift*

Physical characteristics

alto/a	*tall* (m./f.)
bajo/a	*short* (m./f.)
delgado/a	*thin* (m./f.)
gordo/a	*fat* (m./f.)
moreno/a	*dark-haired* (m./f.)
pelirrojo/a	*red-haired* (m./f.)
rubio/a	*blond* (m./f.)

Personality and mood

antipático/a	*unpleasant, mean* (m./f.)
bueno/a	*kind, good* (m./f.)
enfadado/a	*angry* (m./f.)
inteligente	*intelligent*
listo/a	*bright, clever* (m./f.)
malo/a	*bad, mean* (m./f.)
pijo/a	*posh, snobby* (m./f.)
simpático/a	*nice* (m./f.)

The face

la boca	*mouth*
la cara	*face*
el diente	*tooth*
las gafas	*glasses, spectacles*
el labio	*lip*
la lengua	*tongue*
la nariz	*nose*
el ojo	*eye*
la oreja	*ear*
el pelo	*hair*

Expressing opinions

en absoluto	*not at all, absolutely not*
en mi opinión	*in my opinion*
en serio	*seriously, truly*
estoy seguro/a de que	*I'm sure that* (m./f.)
para mi gusto	*for my taste*

Colours

el color	*colour*
amarillo/a	*yellow* (m./f.)
azul	*blue*
blanco/a	*white* (m./f.)
marrón	*brown*
negro/a	*black* (m./f.)
rojo/a	*red* (m./f.)
verde	*green*

Quantifiers

bastante(s)	*enough, quite*
demasiado(s), demasiada(s)	*too much, a lot* (m./f.)

Possessive pronouns

el mío, los míos, la mía, las mías	*mine* (m. sing./pl., f. sing./pl.)
el tuyo, los tuyos, la tuya, las tuyas	*yours* (informal sing.)
el suyo, los suyos, la suya, las suyas	*his, hers, yours* (formal sing.)
el/los nuestro(s), la/las nuestra(s)	*ours*
el/los vuestro(s), la/las vuestra(s)	*yours* (informal pl.)
el suyo, los suyos, la suya, las suyas	*theirs*

Nouns

el cumpleaños	*birthday* Note: **¡Feliz cumpleaños!** *Happy Birthday!*
las ganas	*desire, urge* Note: **tener ganas** *to feel like*
la fiesta	*party, festivity* Note: **¡Felices fiestas!** *Happy holidays!*

ESENCIALES

PAGE 80
Describing characteristics
1 **B** 2 **A** 3 **B** 4 **B**

The face
1 **C** 2 **C** 3 **A** 4 **A** 5 **B** 6 **B**

PAGE 81
Too much, a lot, quite, enough
1 **A** 2 **B** 3 **A** 4 **B** 5 **B** 6 **A** 7 **A** 8 **A** 9 **A** 10 **C** 11 **B** 12 **B**

PAGE 82
To want to, to feel like
1 **B** 2 **B** 3 **A** 4 **C** 5 **B** 6 **B**

PAGE 83
Using the verb *parecer*
1 **C** 2 **B** 3 **B** 4 **A** 5 **B** 6 **C**

PAGE 84
The expression *caer bien / mal*, etc.
1 **A** 2 **A** 3 **B** 4 **B** 5 **B** 6 **A**

Possessive adjectives and pronouns
1 **B** 2 **C** 3 **B** 4 **A** 5 **C**

PAGE 85
Pero (but) or *sino* (but rather, not only ... but)?
1 **A** 2 **B** 3 **A** 4 **B** 5 **C**

Usage of prepositions
1 **B** | 2 **B** | 3 **C** 4 **B** 5 **C** 6 **B**

YOUR
SCORE:

Did you get between 0 and 10? ¡Ay, ay, ay!

Did you get between 11 and 21? Muy justito...

Did you get between 22 and 32? No está mal, pero...

Did you get between 33 and 43? Enhorabuena.

Did you get 44 or over? ¡Eres un auténtico fenómeno!

Tema	**Spelling**

Choose the word that is spelled correctly.

Answers
page 99

1. psychology
   - A psicología
   - B psycología
   - C psychología

2. philosophy
   - A philosophía
   - B filosofía
   - C philosofía

3. physical therapy
   - A physiotherapia
   - B fisiotherapia
   - C fisioterapia

4. gymnastics / calisthenics
   - A gymnasia
   - B gimnasia
   - C gymnasya

5. mathematics
   - A matemáticas
   - B mathemáticas
   - C matemathicas

6. spelling
   - A orthographía
   - B orthografía
   - C ortografía

7. physics
   - A física
   - B fysica
   - C physica

Tema	**School and studies**

Select the most suitable word to complete each sentence.

Answers
page 99

1. ¿A qué hora tienes ... de historia?
   - A curso
   - B clase

2. ¿Vamos a ...?
   - A curso
   - B clase

3. ¿En qué ... estás?
   - A curso
   - B clase

4. El Bachillerato español tiene dos ..., primero y segundo.

   Ⓐ cursos   Ⓑ clases

5. Historia del arte es la ... que más me gusta.

   Ⓐ firma   Ⓑ asignatura

6. Tienes una bonita ...

   Ⓐ firma.   Ⓑ asignatura.

7. Soy más bien de letras y siempre ... matemáticas.

   Ⓐ apruebo   Ⓑ suspendo

8. Y yo soy de ciencias y nunca ... lengua castellana.

   Ⓐ apruebo   Ⓑ suspendo

Tema   **The masculine and neuter article**

Select the correct article or set of articles for each context.

Answers
page 99.

1. No me gusta tu gazpacho, prefiero ... de mi madre.

   Ⓐ el   Ⓑ lo

2. ... bueno de estudiar Historia del arte es que hay muchas chicas.

   Ⓐ El   Ⓑ Lo

3. A ti te encanta el profesor de física y a mí ... de lengua.

   Ⓐ el   Ⓑ lo

4. Mi hermano es ... mejor alumno del instituto.

   Ⓐ el   Ⓑ lo

5. ¿A ti qué es ... que te gusta en la vida?

   Ⓐ el   Ⓑ lo

6. En una película de policías siempre están ... bueno y ... malo.

   Ⓐ el / el   Ⓑ lo / lo   Ⓒ el / lo   Ⓓ lo / el

7. En la vida hay que saber juntar ... útil con ... agradable.

   (A) el / el   (B) lo / lo   (C) el / lo   (D) lo / el

8. ... que se matricula en Medicina sabe ... que hace: una carrera larga y difícil.

   (A) El / el   (B) Lo / lo   (C) El / lo   (D) Lo / el

Tema   **None, some, nothing, something, etc.**

Choose the correct form of the indefinite pronoun or adjective.

Answers page 99

1. No me gusta ... asignatura científica.

   (A) ninguno   (B) ninguna   (C) nadie

2. ... carreras son largas y difíciles.

   (A) Alguna   (B) Algunas   (C) Alguien

3. Todas las semanas visito ... museo.

   (A) algún   (B) alguno   (C) algunos

4. ¿Hay ... aquí?

   (A) ningún   (B) algún   (C) alguien

5. ... días no me puedo levantar.

   (A) Algunas   (B) Algunos   (C) Algún

6. Quiero decirte ...

   (A) algo.   (B) nada.   (C) alguno.

7. ... de mis amigos estudia una carrera científica.

   (A) Ningún   (B) Ninguno   (C) Ninguna

8. No tengo ... amigo médico.

   (A) nadie   (B) ninguno   (C) ningún

9. Siempre veo ... serie antes de acostarme.

   (A) algo   (B) alguien   (C) alguna

Tema   Expressing obligation

For each statement, select the grammatically correct response expressing obligation (to have to, to need to, must, etc.).

1. No tengo buenas notas en letras. / ...

    A   Hay que leas más.

    B   Tienes que leer más.

    C   Tienes leer más.

Answers page 99

2. Mi hermano nunca aprueba Historia. / ...

    A   Tienes que ayudarle.

    B   Hay que le ayudas.

    C   Hay ayudarle.

3. La carrera que les gusta no es fácil. / ...

    A   Tienen estudiar mucho.

    B   Tienen que estudiar mucho.

    C   Hay que estudien mucho.

4. Mi hija quiere dedicarse a la música. / ...

    A   Para eso tiene que tenga talento.

    B   Para eso tiene tener talento.

    C   Para eso hay que tener talento.

5. Estamos siempre cansados. / ...

    A   Hay que acostarse antes.

    B   Tenéis que acostarse antes.

    C   Tenéis acostaros antes.

Unit 10
ESENCIALES

Choose the correct spelling for each progressive tense verb.

Answers page 99

1. ¿Estáis ...?
   - Ⓐ dormiendo
   - Ⓑ duermiendo
   - Ⓒ durmiendo

2. Están ... algo importante.
   - Ⓐ diciendo
   - Ⓑ deciendo
   - Ⓒ dieciendo

3. Esta casa se está ...
   - Ⓐ cayendo.
   - Ⓑ caendo.
   - Ⓒ caiendo.

4. Te estás ... demasiada carne.
   - Ⓐ serviendo
   - Ⓑ sirviendo
   - Ⓒ sirvendo

5. Estoy ... a clase.
   - Ⓐ endo
   - Ⓑ yendo
   - Ⓒ iendo

Tema **Expressing a continuing action**

*To express that something is 'still' being done, a conjugated form of **seguir** + an -ing verb is used. Choose the correct option.*

1. Todavía estudiamos.
   - Ⓐ Seguimos estudiando.
   Answers page 99
   - Ⓑ Siguimos estudiando.
   - Ⓒ Siguemos estudiendo.

2. ¿Todavía creéis en Papá Noel?
   - Ⓐ ¿Seguéis creando en Papá Noel?
   - Ⓑ ¿Seguís creyendo en Papá Noel?
   - Ⓒ ¿Siguís creendo en Papá Noel?

3. A su edad, ¿tienen todavía ganas de salir?
   - Ⓐ ¿Seguen tenando ganas de salir?
   - Ⓑ ¿Seguen tieniendo ganas de salir?
   - Ⓒ ¿Siguen teniendo ganas de salir?

4. Con sesenta años todavía lee cómics.

A Con sesenta años segue leendo cómics.

B Con sesenta años sigue leyendo cómics.

C Con sesenta años sige leando cómics.

5. Con treinta años todavía pido ayuda a mis padres.

A Con treinta años sigo pidiendo ayuda a mis padres.

B Con treinta años siguo pediendo ayuda a mis padres.

C Con treinta años sego pidiendo ayuda a mis padres.

6. ¿Todavía piensas en mí?

A ¿Siges piensando en mí?

B ¿Segues piensando en mí?

C ¿Sigues pensando en mí?

Verbs	ÚTILES
aprobar	*to pass an exam* Note: verb with a spelling change
conseguir	*to get, to obtain* Note: verb with a spelling change
costar	*to cost* (**costar trabajo** *to be difficult*) Note: verb with a spelling change
elegir	*to choose, to select* Note: verb with a spelling change
leer	*to read*
matricularse	*to register, to enrol* (e.g. for a course)
pedir	*to ask for* Note: verb with a spelling change
seguir	*to continue* (+ progressive tense = *to continue to*) Note: verb with a spelling change
suspender	*to fail an exam*

Unit 10
ÚTILES

School and studies

la asignatura	*subject, course*
la filosofía	*philosophy*
la física	*physics*
la gimnasia	*gymnastics, calisthenics, physical exercise*
las matemáticas	*mathematics*
la música	*music*
el bachillerato	*high school diploma, A levels*
la carrera	*university degree*
la clase	*course*
el curso	*school year*
la firma	*signature*
la fisioterapia	*physical therapy*
el instituto	*secondary school*
la medicina	*medicine*
la nota	*grade, mark*
la ortografía	*spelling*
la psicología	*psychology*
ser de letras	*to be literary*
ser de ciencias	*to be scientific*

Indefinite pronouns & adjectives

alguien	*someone*
algo	*something*
algún, alguno, alguna, algunos, algunas	*some, any*
ningún, ninguno, ninguna	*none, not any*

ESENCIALES

PAGE 90

Spelling
1 **A** 2 **B** 3 **C** 4 **B** 5 **A** 6 **C** 7 **A**

School and studies
1 **B** 2 **B** 3 **A** 4 **A** 5 **B** 6 **A** 7 **B** 8 **A**

PAGE 91

The masculine and neuter article
1 **A** 2 **B** 3 **A** 4 **A** 5 **B** 6 **A** 7 **B** 8 **C**

PAGE 92

Some, none, something, nothing, etc.
1 **B** 2 **B** 3 **A** 4 **C** 5 **B** 6 **A** 7 **B** 8 **C** 9 **C**

PAGE 93

Expressing obligation
1 **B** 2 **A** 3 **B** 4 **C** 5 **A**

PAGE 94

Expressing 'to find it hard to'
1 **C** 2 **A** 3 **C** 4 **B** 5 **A** 6 **A**

PAGE 95

Conjugation: verbs with a spelling change
1 **B** 2 **C** 3 **A** 4 **C** 5 **C** 6 **B**
1 **A** 2 **A** 3 **C** 4 **B**

PAGE 96

Irregular -ing verbs
1 **C** 2 **A** 3 **A** 4 **B** 5 **B**

Expressing a continuing action
1 **A** 2 **B** 3 **C** 4 **B** 5 **A** 6 **C**

YOUR SCORE:

Did you get between 0 and 12? ¡Ay, ay, ay!

Did you get between 13 and 25? Muy justito...

Did you get between 26 and 38? No está mal, pero...

Did you get between 39 and 51? Enhorabuena.

Did you get 52 or over? ¡Eres un auténtico fenómeno!

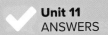

ESENCIALES

PAGE 100

Conjunctions (or / and)
1 **A** | 2 **B** | 3 **B** | 4 **A** | 5 **B**
1 **A** | 2 **B** | 3 **B** | 4 **A** | 5 **A**

. . . .

Giving a price
1 **C** | 2 **B** | 3 **A** | 4 **A**

PAGE 101

Spending and saving
1 **B** | 2 **B** | 3 **A** | 4 **A** | 5 **A**

. . . .

PAGE 102

Expressing necessity
1 **C** | 2 **B** | 3 **C** | 4 **C** | 5 **A** | 6 **B** | 7 **A** | 8 **C**

. . . .

PAGE 103

To learn, to inform, to teach
1 **C** | 2 **B** | 3 **B** | 4 **A** | 5 **A** | 6 **C**

. . . .

Expressing 'to occur to'
1 **B** | 2 **A** | 3 **A** | 4 **C** | 5 **A** | 6 **C**

PAGE 104

Some common expressions
1 **A** | 2 **B** | 3 **A** | 4 **A** | 5 **B** | 6 **B**

. . . .

Porque (because) or *y eso que* (even though)?
1 **B** | 2 **A** | 3 **A** | 4 **B** | 5 **B** | 6 **A**

. . . .

PAGE 105

Conjugation: the verb *oír*
1 **C** | 2 **C** | 3 **B** | 4 **A** | 5 **A** | 6 **B**

YOUR SCORE:

Did you get between **0 and 10?** ¡Ay, ay, ay!

Did you get between **11 and 21?** Muy justito...

Did you get between **22 and 32?** No está mal, pero...

Did you get between **33 and 43?** Enhorabuena.

Did you get **44 or over?** ¡Eres un auténtico fenómeno!

Tema   Asking how things are

There are several ways to ask how someone is or what they've been up to. Choose the appropriate phrase for each question.

1. ¿... de ti?
   - **A** Cómo es
   - **B** Qué es
   - **C** Qué tal es

   Answers page 118

2. ¿... os va?
   - **A** Cómo tal
   - **B** Qué tal
   - **C** Qué

3. ¿... le va a tu marido?
   - **A** Cómo tal
   - **B** Cómo
   - **C** Qué es

4. ¿Qué ... ?
   - **A** ... les va a tus padres?
   - **B** ... están tus padres?
   - **C** ... es de tus padres?

5. ¿Cómo ... ?
   - **A** ... tal te va?
   - **B** ... te va?
   - **C** ... es de ti?

6. ¿Qué ... ?
   - **A** ... estáis?
   - **B** ... os va?
   - **C** ... tal estáis?

Tema   The world of work

Answers page 118

Select the sentence with the same meaning.

1. Soy becario en un periódico.
   - **A** Estoy haciendo prácticas de periodista.
   - **B** Tengo un contrato fijo en un periódico.

2. Estoy en el paro.

   Ⓐ No tengo trabajo.　　　　Ⓑ Tengo un trabajillo.

3. Estoy despedido.

   Ⓐ No estoy contento con mi trabajo.　Ⓑ Pierdo mi empleo.

4. No cobro nada.

   Ⓐ Trabajo gratis.　　　　Ⓑ No tengo experiencia profesional.

5. No me quejo de lo que cobro.

   Ⓐ No tengo un buen salario.　　Ⓑ Estoy contento con mi salario.

Tema *Desde (since) or desde hace (for)?*

Choose the correct option for each case.

Answers page 118

1. Trabajo en esta empresa ... un año.

   Ⓐ desde　　　　　　　Ⓑ desde hace

2. No te veo ... mucho tiempo.

   Ⓐ desde　　　　　　　Ⓑ desde hace

3. Estoy en el paro ... seis meses.

   Ⓐ desde　　　　　　　Ⓑ desde hace

4. Soy panadera ... el año 2015.

   Ⓐ desde　　　　　　　Ⓑ desde hace

5. Estoy cursando Formación Profesional ... septiembre de este año.

   Ⓐ desde　　　　　　　Ⓑ desde hace

6. ¿A qué te dedicas ahora? No sé nada de ti ... el Bachillerato.

   Ⓐ desde　　　　　　　Ⓑ desde hace

7. Estoy de baja ... un mes.

   Ⓐ desde　　　　　　　Ⓑ desde hace

Tema Some common expressions

Choose the most appropriate response to each statement.

Answers page 118

1. Con mi formación de panadero siempre consigo trabajo.

   Ⓐ ¡Vaya rollo!   Ⓑ ¡Qué chulo!

2. Solo consigo contratos cortos de becario.

   Ⓐ ¡Vaya rollo!   Ⓑ ¡Qué chulo!

3. Trabajo mucho y cobro poco.

   Ⓐ ¡Vaya rollo!   Ⓑ ¡Qué chulo!

4. Me va regular con los compañeros en el trabajo.

   Ⓐ ¡Vaya rollo!   Ⓑ ¡Qué chulo!

5. Cuando empiezo a adquirir experiencia, me despiden.

   Ⓐ ¡Vaya rollo!   Ⓑ ¡Qué chulo!

6. Por fin tengo un contrato largo en una empresa.

   Ⓐ ¡Vaya rollo!   Ⓑ ¡Qué chulo!

7. No me puedo quejar, tengo un oficio agradable.

   Ⓐ ¡Vaya rollo!   Ⓑ ¡Qué chulo!

Tema The present perfect

Select the equivalent in the present perfect for each case.

1. ¿Qué carrera estudiáis?

   Ⓐ ¿Qué carrera hais estudiado?

   Answers page 118

   Ⓑ ¿Qué carrera habéis estudiados?

   Ⓒ ¿Qué carrera habéis estudiado?

2. Me despiden del trabajo.

   Ⓐ Me han despedido del trabajo.

   Ⓑ Me han despidido del trabajo.

   Ⓒ Me han despedidos del trabajo.

3. No encuentro prácticas interesantes.

   A No ho encontrado prácticas interesantes.

   B No he encontrado prácticas interesantes.

   C No ho encuentrado prácticas interesantes.

4. No nos quejamos.

   A No nos hemos quejado.

   B No nos habemos quejado.

   C No nos somos quejados.

5. Mi hijo quiere cursar FP.

   A Mi hijo ha quierido cursar FP.

   B Mi hijo ha querado cursar FP:

   C Mi hijo ha querido cursar FP.

6. ¿A qué hora sales, Carmen?

   A ¿A qué hora has salido, Carmen?

   B ¿A qué hora eres salida, Carmen?

   C ¿A qué hora has salida, Carmen?

Choose the correct translation in each case.

Answers
page 118

1. They didn't do anything.

   A No han hacido nada.   C No han hacidas nada.

   B No han hecho nada.

2. Did you see something?

   A ¿Has veído algo ?   C ¿Has visto algo?

   B ¿Has vido algo?

3. They came early.

   A Son venido temprano.   C Han venido temprano.

   B Son venidos temprano.

4. You (pl.) got here too late.

   A Habéis llegado demasiado tarde.   C Sois llegados demasiado tarde.

   B Sois llegado demasiado tarde.

5. Nothing happened.

   A No ha pasado nada.   C No he pasado nada.

   B No es pasado nada.

6. I dropped by your house.

   A He pasada por tu casa.   C Soy pasada por tu casa.

   B He pasado por tu casa.

Tema Commands

Choose the command that expresses the stated obligation.

Answers page 118

1. Tienes que entender a tu hija.

   A Entiéndela.   C Entendedla.

   B Enténdedla.   D Entiendela.

2. Tenéis que contar lo que ha pasado.

   A Cóntalo.   C Cuéntalo.

   B Contadlo.   D Cuentalo.

3. Tenéis que pedir contratos fijos.

   A Pedidlos.   C Pidelos.

   B Pedilos.   D Pídelos.

4. Tienes que conseguir unas prácticas chulas.

   A Conséguelas.   C Consiguedlas.

   B Consíguelas.   D Conseguidlas.

Unit 12
ESENCIALES

Select the command that corresponds to the elements provided.

Answers page 118

1. tú / despertarse
   - A Despertate.
   - B Despértate.
   - C Despiertate.
   - D Despiértate.

2. tú / servirse
   - A Sérvete.
   - B Sírvete.
   - C Siérvete.
   - D Sirvete.

3. tú / seguir esta serie
   - A Síguela.
   - B Siguela.
   - C Seguila.
   - D Séguila.

4. tú / decir / a mí / tu nombre
   - A Dilome.
   - B Dímilo.
   - C Dímelo.
   - D Dílomi.

5. tú / enseñar / a nosotras / los dientes
   - A Enseñálasnos.
   - B Enseñálosnos.
   - C Enseñanoslas.
   - D Enséñanoslos.

6. tú / presentar / a él / tus compañeras
   - A Preséntaselas.
   - B Preséntalelas.
   - C Presentalasle.
   - D Presentáselas.

Tema *Pues, desde and después*

Select the correct translation for each sentence.

Answers page 118

1. Tienes pues que aprender un oficio.
   - A After that you need to learn a profession.
   - B So you need to learn a profession.

2. He aprendido un oficio, pues la carrera no me va a dar trabajo.

   A I've learned a trade since my degree is not going to lead to work.

   B I've learned a trade even though my degree will lead to a good job.

3. Pues he estudiado informática y ahora diseño páginas web.

   A Later, I studied IT and now I design websites.

   B So I studied IT and now I design websites.

4. Desde niño he querido ser panadero.

   A When I was a child I wanted to be a baker.

   B Since I was a child I've wanted to be a baker.

5. Después del Bachillerato no he hecho nada.

   A Since I graduated from secondary school I haven't done anything.

   B After graduating from secondary school I didn't do anything.

Tema Affirmative or negative responses

Select the most appropriate affirmative or negative response in each exchange.

1. ¿Has conseguido un contrato fijo? / ¡...! Trabajillos y nada más.

   A ¡Claro que sí!   B ¡Qué va!

   Answers page 118

2. Están contentos contigo en la empresa, ¿verdad? / ¡...! Me han despedido esta mañana.

   A ¡Claro que sí!   B ¡Qué va!

3. Parece que te va fatal en la Universidad. / ¡...! He aprobado todas las asignaturas.

   A ¡Claro que sí!   B ¡Qué va!

4. En algunos casos las prácticas son interesantes. / ¡...! Yo he aprendido mucho como becario.

   A ¡Claro que sí!   B ¡Qué va!

5. ¿Sabes diseñar páginas web? / ¡...! He cursado la carrera de informática.

   A ¡Claro que sí!   B ¡Qué va!

6. ¿Tienes derecho a cobrar el paro? / ¡...! No es mucho, pero no me quejo.

   A ¡Claro que sí!   **B** ¡Qué va!

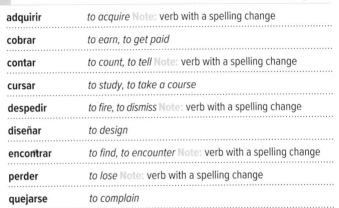

Verbs   ÚTILES

adquirir	*to acquire* Note: verb with a spelling change
cobrar	*to earn, to get paid*
contar	*to count, to tell* Note: verb with a spelling change
cursar	*to study, to take a course*
despedir	*to fire, to dismiss* Note: verb with a spelling change
diseñar	*to design*
encontrar	*to find, to encounter* Note: verb with a spelling change
perder	*to lose* Note: verb with a spelling change
quejarse	*to complain*

Asking and saying how things are

¿Qué es de ti / de vosotros / de Pedro?	*What are you* (informal sing.) / *you* (informal pl.) *up to? / What is Pedro up to?*
¿Cómo (or **Qué tal**) **te va / os va / le va a Pedro?**	*How is everything going with you* (informal sing.) / *you* (informal pl.) / *Pedro?*
Estoy contento/a.	*I'm happy.* (m./f.)
Me va bien / mal.	*Everything is going well / badly.*
No me quejo.	*I can't complain.*
Me ha ido bien.	*Everything went well.*

The world of work

becario/a	*intern* (m./f.)
compañero/a	*coworker, classmate, teammate* (m./f.)

el contrato	*contract*
despedido/a	*a dismissed or laid-off employee* (m./f.)
la empresa	*company*
la experiencia	*experience*
fijo/a	*fixed, permanent* (m./f.)
una formación profesional	*vocational training*
gratis	*free of charge*
la informática	*information technology, computing*
el oficio	*trade, profession*
la página web	*website*
panadero/a	*baker* (m./f.)
el paro	*unemployment*
el periódico	*newspaper*
las prácticas	*internship*
el salario	*salary, wage*

Conjunctions and prepositions

pues	*well ...* (to indicate a consequence) *because, as, since* (to indicate a cause) *so* (to indicate a logical sequence of events)
desde	*since* (date: **Desde 1950 ...** *Since 1950 ...*)
desde hace	*for* (duration: **Desde hace una semana ...** *For a week ...*)

Some common expressions

¡Qué rollo! / ¡Vaya rollo!	*What a pain!*
¡Qué chulo!	*How great!*
¡Qué va!	*No way!*

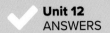

Unit 12
ANSWERS

ESENCIALES

PAGE 109

Asking how things are

1 **B** 2 **B** 3 **B** 4 **C** 5 **B** 6 **C**

The world of work

1 **A** 2 **A** 3 **B** 4 **A** 5 **B**

PAGE 110

Desde (since) or *desde hace* (for)?

1 **B** 2 **B** 3 **B** 4 **A** 5 **A** 6 **A** 7 **B**

PAGE 111

Some common expressions

1 **B** 2 **A** 3 **A** 4 **A** 5 **A** 6 **B** 7 **B**

The present perfect

1 **C** 2 **A** 3 **B** 4 **A** 5 **C** 6 **A**

1 **B** 2 **C** 3 **C** 4 **A** 5 **A** 6 **B**

PAGE 113

Commands

1 **A** 2 **B** 3 **A** 4 **B**

1 **D** 2 **B** 3 **A** 4 **C** 5 **D** 6 **A**

PAGE 114

Pues, desde and *después*

1 **B** 2 **A** 3 **B** 4 **B** 5 **B**

PAGE 115

Affirmative and negative responses

1 **B** 2 **B** 3 **B** 4 **A** 5 **A** 6 **A**

Did you get between 0 and 11? ¡Ay, ay, ay!

Did you get between 12 and 22? Muy justito...

Did you get between 23 and 33? No está mal, pero...

Did you get between 34 and 44? Enhorabuena.

Did you get 45 or over? ¡Eres un auténtico fenómeno!

Tema **Clothing**

In these sentences, the term related to clothing is missing its ending. Select the ending to complete the word.

1. Para salir de noche lo más elegante es una fal... larga.

Answers page 128

   A ...seta   B ...dora   C ...tivas   D ...da

   E ...pa   F ...queros   G ...patos

2. Me gasto todo el dinero en las tiendas de ro...

   A ...seta.   B ...dora.   C ...tivas.   D ...da.

   E ...pa.   F ...queros.   G ...patos.

3. Tengo veinte pares de za...

   A ...seta.   B ...dora.   C ...tivas.   D ...da.

   E ...pa.   F ...queros.   G ...patos.

4. Me he comprado una cami... de la Universidad.

   A ...seta   B ...dora   C ...tivas   D ...da

   E ...pa   F ...queros   G ...patos

5. Es un viejo rockero: siempre lleva caza... de cuero.

   A ...seta   B ...dora   C ...tivas   D ...da

   E ...pa   F ...queros   G ...patos

6. Yo solo me pongo va... azules.

   A ...seta   B ...dora   C ...tivas   D ...da

   E ...pa   F ...queros   G ...patos

7. Algunas depor... son carísimas.

   A ...seta   B ...dora   C ...tivas   D ...da

   E ...pa   F ...queros   G ...patos

Now the term related to clothing is missing its beginning. Select the beginning to complete the word.

Answers page 128

1. Hola, ¿tienen ...canas azules?

   Ⓐ cami... Ⓑ tra... Ⓒ ves... Ⓓ chán...

   Ⓔ ameri... Ⓕ cha.., Ⓖ panta...

2. En mi colegio todos los alumnos llevan ...dal.

   Ⓐ cami... Ⓑ tra... Ⓒ ves... Ⓓ chán...

   Ⓔ ameri... Ⓕ cha... Ⓖ panta...

3. Busco una ...sa blanca talla 44.

   Ⓐ cami... Ⓑ tra... Ⓒ ves... Ⓓ chán...

   Ⓔ ameri... Ⓕ cha... Ⓖ panta...

4. ¿Dónde está mi ...lón corto?

   Ⓐ cami... Ⓑ tra... Ⓒ ves... Ⓓ chán...

   Ⓔ ameri... Ⓕ cha... Ⓖ panta...

5. Para ir a la ópera hay que ponerse un ...je.

   Ⓐ cami... Ⓑ tra... Ⓒ ves... Ⓓ chán...

   Ⓔ ameri... Ⓕ cha... Ⓖ panta...

6. ¿Dónde has comprado ese ...tido tan bonito?

   Ⓐ cami... Ⓑ tra... Ⓒ ves... Ⓓ chán...

   Ⓔ ameri... Ⓕ cha... Ⓖ panta...

7. Esta ...queta está sucia.

   Ⓐ cami... Ⓑ tra... Ⓒ ves... Ⓓ chán...

   Ⓔ ameri... Ⓕ cha... Ⓖ panta...

Tema **Job interview**

Choose the option that conveys the same idea as the statement or question provided.

1. Tengo cita para un trabajo.

   (A) Estoy capacitado para este trabajo.

   (B) Vengo a una entrevista de trabajo.

Answers
page 128

2. Tengo trabajos eventuales.

   (A) Trabajo algunos meses al año.

   (B) Trabajo en una empresa que organiza congresos y reuniones.

3. Es un trabajo cara al público.

   (A) Hay que atender directamente al cliente.

   (B) Hay muchos candidatos para este trabajo.

4. ¿Cuándo me incorporo?

   (A) ¿Cuánto voy a cobrar?

   (B) ¿Cuándo empiezo a trabajar?

Select the most appropriate reply in each of these exchanges.

Answers
page 128

1. Me apasiona la moda. / [...] buscamos empleados motivados.

   (A) Perfecto,   (B) Está muy bien, pero

2. La ilusión de mi vida es trabajar para ustedes. / [...] usted no tiene experiencia.

   (A) Perfecto, pero   (B) Está muy bien,

3. Ya he trabajado cara al público, en un bar. / [...] esto es diferente: es una tienda de ropa.

   (A) Ya, pero   (B) Está muy bien,

4. He contestado a su anuncio porque necesito un trabajillo. / [...] no queremos becarios.

   (A) Perfecto, pero   (B) Está muy bien,

Unit 13
ESENCIALES

How did the interview go? Select the positive or negative response according to the rest of the answer.

1. [...] Es usted demasiado joven para este puesto.

   Ⓐ Enhorabuena, su candidatura me ha convencido.

   Ⓑ Lo siento, su perfil no es exactamente el que buscamos.

Answers page 128

2. [...] ¿Cuándo puede usted incorporarse?

   Ⓐ Enhorabuena, su candidatura me ha convencido.

   Ⓑ Lo siento, su perfil no es exactamente el que buscamos.

3. [...] Dígame qué sueldo le parece bien para empezar.

   Ⓐ Enhorabuena, su candidatura me ha convencido.

   Ⓑ Lo siento, su perfil no es exactamente el que buscamos.

4. [...] Necesitamos personas con otro tipo de currículum.

   Ⓐ Enhorabuena, su candidatura me ha convencido.

   Ⓑ Lo siento, su perfil no es exactamente el que buscamos.

Tema **Expressions with the verb *dar***

*Select the correct construction of **dar igual** (to not matter to one, to be indifferent) that corresponds to each statement.*

1. The salary doesn't matter to me.

   Ⓐ Me da igual el sueldo.

   Ⓑ Me doy igual el sueldo.

Answers page 128

2. My friends don't care about the clothes they wear.

   Ⓐ A mis amigos se dan igual la ropa que llevan.

   Ⓑ A mis amigos les da igual la ropa que llevan.

3. Blue, green or black, the colours make no difference to us.

   Ⓐ Azul, verde o negro, nos dan igual los colores.

   Ⓑ Azul, verde o negro, nos damos igual los colores.

4. I prefer Tuesday, if it doesn't matter to you.

   Ⓐ Prefiero el martes, si te das igual.

   Ⓑ Prefiero el martes, si te da igual.

5. If it's all the same to you, let's see each other tomorrow.

   Ⓐ Si os da igual, nos vemos mañana.

   Ⓑ Si os dais igual, nos vemos mañana.

---

*Select the correct construction of **darse cuenta** (to realize, to become aware) that corresponds to each statement.*

1. Do you (formal sing.) realize what you're saying?

   Ⓐ ¿Le da usted cuenta de lo que dice?

   Ⓑ ¿Se da usted cuenta de lo que dice?

Answers page 128

2. Excuse me, I didn't realize.

   Ⓐ Disculpe, no me he dado cuenta.

   Ⓑ Disculpe, no me ha dado cuenta.

3. I don't understand anything.

   Ⓐ No me doy cuenta de nada.

   Ⓑ No me da cuenta de nada.

4. You (informal pl.) are not aware of certain things.

   Ⓐ No os dan cuenta de algunas cosas.

   Ⓑ No os dais cuenta de algunas cosas.

5. Many customers do not realize that it is expensive.

   Ⓐ Muchos clientes no les dan cuenta de que es caro.

   Ⓑ Muchos clientes no se dan cuenta de que es caro.

6. We did not realize what time it was.

   Ⓐ No nos hemos dado cuenta de la hora.

   Ⓑ No nos ha dado cuenta de la hora.

Unit 13
ESENCIALES

Tema Adverbs

*Select the correct form of the adverb ending in **-mente** in each case.*

1. Estoy ... de acuerdo con usted.

    Ⓐ enteromente　　　　　Ⓑ enteramente

Answers page 128

2. No es usted ... el tipo de empleado que buscamos.

    Ⓐ exactomente　　　　　Ⓑ exactamente

3. Hay que atender ... al cliente.

    Ⓐ amablemente　　　　　Ⓑ amablamente

4. Aprendo idiomas muy ...

    Ⓐ fácilmente.　　　　　Ⓑ fácilamente.

5. ... para usted, nuestros clientes son bastante simpáticos.

    Ⓐ Felizamente　　　　　Ⓑ Felizmente

6. ... tengo un trabajo de camarero.

    Ⓐ Actualmente　　　　　Ⓑ Actualamente

Tema *El / lo*: the masculine and neuter article

Choose the correct option to complete each sentence.

Answers page 128

1. ¿Qué es ... en la vida?

    Ⓐ el tuyo　　　　　Ⓑ lo tuyo

2. ... es trabajar en la moda.

    Ⓐ El mío　　　　　Ⓑ Lo mío

3. ... la camisa blanca es mi hermano.

    Ⓐ El de　　　　　Ⓑ Lo de

4. ... hacerme un tatuaje no me convence.

    Ⓐ El de　　　　　Ⓑ Lo de

5. ¿... sueldo es importante para usted?

    Ⓐ El del　　　　　Ⓑ Lo del

6. El nuevo dependiente es ... pelo largo.

   Ⓐ el del

   Ⓑ lo del

7. ¡Este chándal es ... !

   Ⓐ el mío

   Ⓑ lo mío

8. Mi vestido es clásico y ... es moderno.

   Ⓐ el suyo

   Ⓑ lo suyo

Tema **The present perfect**

Choose the equivalent conveyed in the present perfect.

1. ¿Por qué te vistes así, Julia?

   Ⓐ ¿Por qué te has vestido así, Julia?

   Ⓑ ¿Por qué te has vistido así, Julia?

   Ⓒ ¿Por qué te eres vistida así, Julia?

Answers page 128

2. No te decimos nada.

   Ⓐ No te hemos dicho nada.

   Ⓑ No te hemos decidos nada.

   Ⓒ No te hemos dichos nada.

3. Siempre soy amable con la gente.

   Ⓐ Siempre he seído amable con la gente.

   Ⓑ Siempre soy sido amable con la gente.

   Ⓒ Siempre he sido amable con la gente.

4. ¿No os ponéis el traje?

   Ⓐ ¿No os habéis posto el traje?

   Ⓑ ¿No os habéis puesto el traje?

   Ⓒ ¿No os habéis puestos el traje?

Unit 13
ÚTILES

Verbs

apasionar	*to be passionate about*
atender	*to attend to, to help customers* Note: verb with a spelling change
contestar	*to answer, to reply*
convencer	*to convince*
dar	*to give*
dar igual	*to not matter to one, to be indifferent to*
darse cuenta	*to realize, to be aware*
incorporarse	*to be recruited for a position*
poner	*to put* Note: the reflexive verb **ponerse** is used for putting on clothes.
vestirse	*to get dressed* Note: verb with a spelling change

Clothing

la americana	*blazer, sport coat*
la camisa	*shirt*
la camiseta	*T-shirt*
la cazadora	*leather or denim jacket, bomber jacket*
el chándal	*track suit, sweatsuit*
la chaqueta	*suit jacket*
las deportivas	*trainers, tennis shoes*
la falda	*skirt*
el pantalón	*trousers* Note: this word is often singular in Spanish.
la ropa	*clothes* Note: this word is singular in Spanish.
el traje	*suit*
los vaqueros	*jeans* Note: **el vaquero** means *cowboy*.

| el vestido | dress |
| los zapatos | shoes |

Job interview

el anuncio	advertisement
candidato/a	candidate (m./f.)
la candidatura	application
capacitado/a	trained, qualified (m./f.)
cara al público	public facing
la cita	appointment, meeting
cliente/a	customer, client (m./f.)
el currículum	CV
dependiente/a	salesperson (m./f.)
la entrevista	interview
eventual	temporary, casual
la experiencia	experience
la gente	people
la ilusión	dream
la moda	fashion, style
motivado/a	motivated (m./f.)
el perfil	profile
el puesto	post, position
el sueldo	salary
la tienda	shop, store

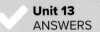

Unit 13
ANSWERS

ESENCIALES

PAGE 119
Clothing
1 **D** 2 **E** 3 **G** 4 **A** 5 **B** 6 **F** 7 **C**
1 **E** 2 **D** 3 **A** 4 **G** 5 **B** 6 **C** 7 **F**

PAGE 121
Job interview
1 **B** 2 **A** 3 **A** 4 **B**
1 **A** 2 **A** 3 **A** 4 **A**
1 **B** 2 **A** 3 **A** 4 **B**

PAGE 122
Expressions with the verb *dar*
1 **A** 2 **B** 3 **A** 4 **B** 5 **A**
1 **B** 2 **A** 3 **A** 4 **B** 5 **B** 6 **A**

PAGE 124
Adverbs
1 **B** 2 **B** 3 **A** 4 **A** 5 **B** 6 **A**

El / lo: the masculine and neuter article
1 **B** 2 **B** 3 **A** 4 **B** 5 **B** 6 **A** 7 **A** 8 **A**

PAGE 125
The present perfect
1 **A** 2 **A** 3 **C** 4 **B**

Did you get between 0 and 10? ¡Ay, ay, ay!

Did you get between 11 and 21? Muy justito...

Did you get between 22 and 32? No está mal, pero...

Did you get between 33 and 43? Enhorabuena.

Did you get 44 or over? ¡Eres un auténtico fenómeno!

Tema Business and work

Choose the most suitable phrase to complete each sentence.

1. No me entiendo bien con ...
   A mi jeque.
   B mi jefe.

Answers page 138

2. Tengo un trabajo ...
   A de oficio.
   B de oficina.

3. Ha montado un buen ...
   A negocio.
   B negociador.

4. Nuestra empresa atraviesa ...
   A una grave crisis.
   B una grave crisa.

5. Para un comercio en línea no se necesita ...
   A mucha investidura.
   B mucha inversión.

6. Hay ... de distribución.
   A pocos costes
   B pocas cuestas

7. Trabajamos para ... extranjero.
   A el mercedes
   C el mercado

8. Internet abre ... a las empresas.
   A nuevas oportunidades
   B nuevas importunidades

Tema Things could be better ...

Select the statement in Spanish that has the same meaning as the statement in English.

1. You don't look very well.
   A Tienes mala cabeza.
   B Tienes mala cara.

Answers page 138

2. I don't feel comfortable.
   A No estoy a gusto.
   B Estoy de baja.

3. I can't take any more.
   A No puedo no más.
   B No puedo más.

4. I can't stand my colleagues.

   Ⓐ No aguanto a mis compañeros.   Ⓑ Horrorizo a mis compañeros.

5. We are fed up.

   Ⓐ Estamos hartos.   Ⓑ Estamos bastantes.

6. She is burned out.

   Ⓐ Es quemada.   Ⓑ Está quemada.

7. I'm on sick leave.

   Ⓐ Estoy en paro.   Ⓑ Estoy de baja.

Tema *Hay, estar or hace?*

Choose the correct word to complete each sentence.

Answers
page 138

1. ... una reunión a las tres.

   Ⓐ Hay   Ⓑ Está   Ⓒ Hace

2. ... tus compañeros en el despacho.

   Ⓐ Hay   Ⓑ Están   Ⓒ Hacen

3. ... dos soluciones.

   Ⓐ Hay   Ⓑ Están   Ⓒ Hacen

4. ... el director, ¿qué hacemos?

   Ⓐ Hay   Ⓑ Está   Ⓒ Hace

5. Entre mis ciudades preferidas ... Madrid.

   Ⓐ hay   Ⓑ está   Ⓒ hace

6. ¿... alguien?

   Ⓐ Hay   Ⓑ Está   Ⓒ Hace

7. Si en la reunión ... Antonio, yo no voy.

   Ⓐ hay   Ⓑ está   Ⓒ hace

8. Si quieres evitar intermediarios ... la Red.

   Ⓐ hay   Ⓑ está   Ⓒ hace

9. ... otros tipos de comercios menos tradicionales.

   (A) Hay   (B) Están   (C) Hacen

10. He llegado ... una hora.

   (A) hay   (B) está   (C) hace

11. No ... ninguna idea nueva.

   (A) hay   (B) está   (C) hace

12. ... dos años que trabajo en esta empresa.

   (A) Hay   (B) Está   (C) Hace

Tema Here, there, over there

*Choose the most appropriate adverb(s) of place for each context (**aquí** here,
ahí there, **allí** over there).*

1. Estoy ..., en casa, ¿pasa algo?

   (A) aquí   (B) ahí   (C) allí

**Answers
page 138**

2. Mi primo que vive en Estados Unidos me dice que ... es fácil abrir una empresa.

   (A) aquí   (B) ahí   (C) allí

3. ..., en España, tenemos un aceite de oliva bueno y barato.

   (A) Aquí   (B) Ahí   (C) Allí

4. Ponga su firma ..., en ese documento.

   (A) aquí   (B) ahí   (C) allí

5. ¿Qué es esa cosa que llevas ... ?

   (A) aquí   (B) ahí   (C) allí

6. Sé que ..., en el extranjero, hay más trabajo, pero prefiero quedarme ..., en España.

   (A) allí / aquí   (B) aquí / allí   (C) allí / ahí

   (D) ahí / allí   (E) aquí / aquí

Unit 14
ESENCIALES

Tema	**Short-form adjectives**

Choose the correct form of the adjective for each context.

Answers page 138

1. Es mi ... día de trabajo.

   Ⓐ tercera   Ⓑ tercero   Ⓒ tercer

2. Martes es ... día para salir.

   Ⓐ malo   Ⓑ mal   Ⓒ mala

3. No estoy en ... red social.

   Ⓐ ningún   Ⓑ ninguno   Ⓒ ninguna

4. No hay ... comercio en esta calle.

   Ⓐ ningún   Ⓑ ninguno   Ⓒ ninguna

5. El agua es ... para la salud.

   Ⓐ buen   Ⓑ bueno   Ⓒ buena

6. Eres una ... compañera.

   Ⓐ mal   Ⓑ malo   Ⓒ mala

7. Mi empresa es ... del sector.

   Ⓐ tercero   Ⓑ tercera   Ⓒ tercer

8. Es mi ... cita con ella.

   Ⓐ primer   Ⓑ primero   Ⓒ primera

9. ¿Hay ... problema?

   Ⓐ algún   Ⓑ alguno   Ⓒ alguna

10. Es el ... momento.

    Ⓐ buen   Ⓑ bueno   Ⓒ buena

11. De los tres, te gusta ...?

    Ⓐ algún   Ⓑ alguno   Ⓒ alguna

12. Es mi ... empleo.

    Ⓐ primer   Ⓑ primero   Ⓒ primera

Tema	**Verbs ending in -uir: concluir, construir, destruir, distribuir, huir**

Select the correct form of the conjugated verb to complete each sentence.

1. ... nuestros productos en varios países.

    Ⓐ Distribuyimos   Ⓒ Distruibimos

    Ⓑ Distribuimos

    Answers page 138

2. Si ... a través de Internet ahorras bastante.

    Ⓐ distribuyes   Ⓒ distribues

    Ⓑ distribuies

3. Se ... demasiadas casas en la costa.

    Ⓐ construen   Ⓒ construyen

    Ⓑ construien

4. Internet crea empleos, pero también los ...

    Ⓐ destruye.   Ⓒ destruie.

    Ⓑ destrue.

5. ... que no eres feliz en esta empresa.

    Ⓐ Concluo   Ⓒ Concluyo

    Ⓑ Concluio

6. No soportáis las reuniones : cuando hay una, ...

    Ⓐ huyís.   Ⓒ hiuís.

    Ⓑ huis.

Tema	**The present subjunctive**

Select the correct form of the verb to complete each sentence.

Answers page 138

1. Quiero que ... esta carta.

    Ⓐ quemes   Ⓑ quemas

2. No quiero que ... tanto dinero.

    Ⓐ gastáis   Ⓑ gastéis

3. Quiero que mis padres me ...

   Ⓐ comprenden.   Ⓑ comprendan.

4. Quiero que usted me ...

   Ⓐ llama.   Ⓑ llame.

5. Quiero que ... de tú.

   Ⓐ nos tratamos   Ⓑ nos tratemos

6. No quiero que ... aquí.

   Ⓐ vivamos   Ⓑ vivimos

7. No quiero que ... nada malo.

   Ⓐ ocurra   Ⓑ ocurre

8. Quiero que ... la merienda.

   Ⓐ compartéis   Ⓑ compartáis

9. Quiero que me ... más.

   Ⓐ escribas   Ⓑ escribes

10. Mi mujer no quiere que ...

    Ⓐ bebo.   Ⓑ beba.

11. Mis hijos no quieren que ... carne.

    Ⓐ coma   Ⓑ come

12. El profesor quiere que sus alumnos ...

    Ⓐ lean.   Ⓑ leen.

Select the correct form of the verb to complete each sentence.

Answer page 13

1. Voy a levantarme antes de que ... el sol.

   Ⓐ sale   Ⓑ sala   Ⓒ salga   Ⓓ salgue

2. Hago las cosas antes de que me lo ...

   Ⓐ diguan.   Ⓑ digan.   Ⓒ dicen.   Ⓓ diguen.

3. Te pido que ... lo antes posible.

  A venias   B vengues   C venges   D vengas

4. Mis padres siempre me piden que ... yo la mesa.

  A pona   B ponga   C pongue   D pone

Select the statement in the subjunctive that corresponds to the command.

1. Tened una buena formación.

  A Quiero que tenáis una buena formación.

  B Quiero que tenguéis una buena formación.

  C Quiero que tengáis una buena formación.

Answers page 138

2. Sed prudentes.

  A Os pido que seáis prudentes.

  B Os pido que séis prudentes.

  C Os pido que siáis prudentes.

3. Construye una bonita casa.

  A Quiero que construas una bonita casa.

  B Quiero que construyas una bonita casa.

  C Quiero que construes una bonita casa.

4. Perdóname.

  A Te pido que me perdonas.

  B Os pido que me perdonéis.

  C Te pido que me perdones.

Tema Expressing obligation and necessity

The following sentences use different ways to convey obligation or necessity.
Select the word(s) that are missing.

1. Hay que ... a los compañeros.

  A soportar   B soporto   C soporte

Answers page 138

2. No hay que ... en el trabajo.

A te quemas   B te quemes   C quemarse

3. ¿Hace falta ... cucharas?

A que pona   B que pongo   C poner

4. No hace falta que ...

A creerme.   B me creas.   C me crees.

5. Hace falta... diferentes opiniones.

A oír   B que oyas   C que oigues

6. Hace falta que ... más.

A ahorrar   B ahorramos   C ahorremos

7. Hay que ... al jefe.

A aguantes   B aguantas   C aguantar

8. Hay que ... prisa.

A darse   B te des   C te das

Verbs	ÚTILES
abrir	*to open*
aguantar	*to put up with, to endure, to bear*
atravesar	*to cross, to traverse* Note: verb with a spelling change
comprender	*to understand*
concluir	*to conclude*
construir	*to construct, to build*
crear	*to create*
destruir	*to destroy*
distribuir	*to distribute*

huir	*to escape, to flee*
montar	*to mount, to set up (e.g. a business)*
quemar	*to burn*
soportar	*to support, to put up with*

Expressions

darse prisa	*to be in a hurry*

Business and work

el comercio	*shop, business*
el coste	*cost, price*
la crisis	*crisis*
el despacho	*office, study*
en línea	*online*
el extranjero	*abroad*
intermediario/a	*intermediary* (m./f.)
la inversión	*investment*
jefe / jefa	*boss, head* (m./f.)
el mercado	*market*
el negocio	*business deal*
la oficina	*office*
la oportunidad	*opportunity, chance*
el producto	*product*
la red	*network*
la reunión	*meeting*
el sector	*sector*

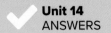

Unit 14
ANSWERS

ESENCIALES

PAGE 129
Business and work
1 **B** 2 **B** 3 **A** 4 **A** 5 **B** 6 **A** 7 **B** 8 **A**

Things could be better ...
1 **B** 2 **A** 3 **B** 4 **A** 5 **A** 6 **D** 7 **D**

PAGE 130
Hay, *estar* or *hace*?
1 **A** 2 **B** 3 **A** 4 **B** 5 **B** 6 **A** 7 **B** 8 **B** 9 **A** 10 **C** 11 **A** 12 **C**

PAGE 131
Here, there, over there
1 **A** 2 **C** 3 **A** 4 **B** 5 **B** 6 **A**

PAGE 132
Short-form adjectives
1 **C** 2 **B** 3 **C** 4 **A** 5 **C** 6 **C** 7 **B** 8 **C** 9 **A** 10 **A** 11 **B** 12 **A**

PAGE 133
Verbs ending in *-uir*: *concluir, construir, destruir, distribuir, huir*
1 **B** 2 **A** 3 **C** 4 **A** 5 **C** 6 **B**

The present subjunctive
1 **A** 2 **B** 3 **B** 4 **B** 5 **B** 6 **A** 7 **A** 8 **B** 9 **A** 10 **B** 11 **A** 12 **A**
1 **C** 2 **B** 3 **D** 4 **B**
1 **C** 2 **A** 3 **B** 4 **C**

PAGE 136
Expressing obligation and necessity
1 **A** 2 **C** 3 **C** 4 **B** 5 **A** 6 **C** 7 **C** 8 **A**

YOUR SCORE:

Did you get between 0 and 15? ¡Ay, ay, ay!

Did you get between 16 and 31? Muy justito...

Did you get between 32 and 47? No está mal, pero...

Did you get between 48 and 63? Enhorabuena.

Did you get 64 or over? ¡Eres un auténtico fenómeno!

Tema Asking directions

For each verb used to indicate directions, select the Spanish equivalent(s). More than one may be correct.

Answers page 147

1. to take
   - **A** poner
   - **B** tomar
   - **C** coger
   - **D** volver

2. to turn
   - **A** doblar
   - **B** girar
   - **C** torcer
   - **D** seguir

3. to continue
   - **A** buscar
   - **B** volver
   - **C** llevar
   - **D** seguir

4. to cross
   - **A** travesar
   - **B** atravesar
   - **C** cruzar
   - **D** subir

Here is some more vocabulary related to giving directions. Select the Spanish equivalent(s). More than one may be correct.

Answers page 147

1. to the left
   - **A** a mano izquierda
   - **B** a pie izquierdo
   - **C** a mano derecha
   - **D** a pie derecho

2. to the right
   - **A** a mano izquierda
   - **B** a pie izquierdo
   - **C** a mano derecha
   - **D** a pie derecho

3. straight on
   - **A** todo derecho
   - **B** todo recto
   - **C** toda derecha
   - **D** toda recta

4. the next
   - **A** la última
   - **B** la cercana
   - **C** la próxima
   - **D** la siguiente

5. up to, until
   - **A** desde
   - **B** en medio
   - **C** hacia
   - **D** hasta

6. near
   - **A** cerca
   - **B** durante
   - **C** sobre todo
   - **D** este

ESENCIALES

---

7. far

- **A** más bien
- **B** lado
- **C** lejos
- **D** entonces

---

*Select the **tú** form to complete each informal command.*

1. ... a la derecha.
   - **A** Gire
   - **B** Gira

Answers page 147

2. ... la plaza.
   - **A** Cruza
   - **B** Cruca
   - **C** Cruce
   - **D** Cruze

3. ... por esta avenida.
   - **A** Sigua
   - **B** Siga
   - **C** Sigue
   - **D** Segue

4. ... la calle.
   - **A** Atravese
   - **B** Atraviese
   - **C** Atravesa
   - **D** Atraviesa

---

*Now select the **usted** form for each formal command giving directions.*

1. ... la primera a la derecha.
   - **A** Toma
   - **B** Tome

Answers page 147

2. ... a la izquierda.
   - **A** Doble
   - **B** Dobla

3. ... la tercera a la derecha.
   - **A** Coja
   - **B** Coga
   - **C** Coje
   - **D** Coge

4. ... por la segunda a la izquierda.
   - **A** Tuerce
   - **B** Tuerza
   - **C** Torce
   - **D** Torza

Tema   Test your vocabulary

Find the odd one out in each set of terms related to the street or to art.

Answers page 147

1.
   - A paso de cebra
   - B acera
   - C paso de peatones
   - D prohibido a los perros

2.
   - A semáforo
   - B fuente
   - C rojo
   - D verde

3.
   - A esquina
   - B bocacalle
   - C naranja
   - D manzana

4.
   - A calzada
   - B carretera
   - C peatón
   - D carril bici

5.
   - A Santiago Bernabéu
   - B Reina Sofía
   - C El Prado
   - D museo

6.
   - A Dalí
   - B Picasso
   - C Cervantes
   - D Miró

7.
   - A mesa
   - B pintura
   - C cuadro
   - D retrato

8.
   - A Guernica
   - B Las señoritas de Aviñón
   - C Mujeres al borde de un ataque de nervios
   - D Las Meninas

Tema   Degrees of distance

Choose the correct form of 'that/those (over there)' for each context.

1. ¿Te acuerdas de ... museo?
   - A aquel
   - B aquello
   - C aquella

Answers page 147

2. ¿Tengo que andar hasta ... fuente?

   A aquel   B aquello   C aquella

3. ¿Sabes qué es ...?

   A aquel   B aquello   C aquella

4. ¿Conoces a ... tipos?

   A aquel   B aquellos   C aquella

5. Me acuerdo de ... cenas de Navidad.

   A aquel   B aquello   C aquellas

Choose the term that conveys the correct degree of distance in each case.

Answers page 147

1. ... que tú dices no me convence.

   A Esto   B Eso   C Aquello

2. ¿Ves aquel hombre, ... a lo lejos?

   A aquí   B ahí   C allí

3. Hola, buenos días, ¡estamos ...!

   A aquí   B ahí   C allí

4. Tus gafas están ..., a tu lado, ¿no las ves?

   A aquí   B ahí   C allí

5. Tiene que seguir hasta ... plaza, allí.

   A esa   B esta   C aquella

6. ... cuadros que a ti te gustan, a mí me horrorizan.

   A Esos   B Estos   C Aquellos

7. Aquí dejo ..., ¿vale?

   A eso   B esto   C aquello

8. Yo nací en 1950. ... era *(it was)* otro mundo.

   A Esto   B Eso   C Aquello

9. En ... tiempo no había *(there were no)* móviles.

   A este   B ese   C aquel

10. ¿Cómo se llama ... pintor del que siempre me hablas?

   A este   B ese   C aquel

11. ... cuadro está bien aquí.

   A Este   B Ese   C Aquel

12. Camarero, ... gambas no están buenas.

   A estas   B esas   C aquellas

Tema Expressing doubt and certainty

Select the term that best describes what each statement conveys.

1. Estoy absolutamente convencido de que el restaurante está cerca de aquí.

   A doubt   B certainty

2. No me cabe la menor duda de que lo vas a conseguir.

   A doubt   B certainty

Answers page 147

3. No estoy en absoluto seguro de lo que digo.

   A doubt   B certainty

4. Estoy segurísimo de que estás equivocado.

   A doubt   B certainty

5. Sé que es verdad.

   A doubt   B certainty

6. Lo dudo mucho.

   A doubt   B certainty

7. Quién sabe si tiene dinero o no.

   A doubt   B certainty

8. Supongo que es a la izquierda.

   A doubt   B certainty

9. A la derecha, por supuesto.

   A doubt   B certainty

Select the option that restates the declaration as a possibility.

Answers page 147

1. Son mis dos museos preferidos.

   A Tal vez sean mis dos museos preferidos.

   B Tal vez esan mis dos museos preferidos.

2. Le da igual ir a uno u otro museo.

   A Puede que le da igual ir a uno u otro museo.

   B Puede que le dé igual ir a uno u otro museo.

3. Vamos a Madrid este fin de semana.

   A Quizás vemos a Madrid este fin de semana.

   B Quizás vayamos a Madrid este fin de semana.

4. Le hago una visita a la abuela.

   A A lo mejor le hagua una visita a la abuela.

   B A lo mejor le hago una visita a la abuela.

5. Voy a visitarte el próximo jueves.

   A Puede ser que vaya a visitarte el próximo jueves.

   B Puede ser que voy a visitarte el próximo jueves.

Tema	**Comprehension and translation**

Choose the correct translation in each case.

Answers page 147

1. No me suena tu cara.

   A You don't look familiar to me.

   B It doesn't seem like you care.

2. Es más bien moderno.

   A It's quite modern.

   B Modern would be much better.

3. ¿Queda cerca la cita?

   A Is the meeting still planned?

   B Is the meeting near here?

4. Me das igual.

   Ⓐ I'm not interested in you.

   Ⓑ You're not interested in me.

5. Where is your house? (i.e. in which area, which way)

   Ⓐ ¿Por dónde queda tu casa?

   Ⓑ ¿En qué esquina está tu casa?

6. I'm never in a hurry.

   Ⓐ Nunca estoy prisa.

   Ⓑ Nunca tengo prisa.

7. I am also an artist.

   Ⓐ Mí también soy artista.

   Ⓑ Yo también soy artista.

Verbs and expressions

ÚTILES

acordarse	*to remember* Note: verb with a spelling change
andar	*to walk*
dudar	*to doubt*
quedar	*to be located*
recordar	*to remember* Note: verb with a spelling change
sonar	*to ring* Note: verb with a spelling change (**me suena** *that rings a bell*, **no me suena** *that doesn't ring a bell*)
suponer	*to suppose* Note: **-go** verb
No cabe duda.	*There is no doubt.*
No me cabe duda.	*I have no doubt.*
No me cabe la menor duda.	*I don't have the slightest doubt.*
tener prisa	*to be in a hurry*

Unit 15
ÚTILES

Directions

al lado	*next to, beside*
cercano/a	*nearby* (m./f.)
durante	*during*
en medio	*in the middle*
hacia	*towards*
¿por dónde...?	*whereabouts?, which way?*
primero/a	*first* (m./f.)
segundo/a	*second* (m./f.)
siguiente	*next*
tercero/a	*third* (m./f.)
último/a	*last* (m./f.)

Around town

la calzada	*road, pavement, sidewalk*
la carretera	*road*
el carril bici	*bicycle path*
la fuente	*fountain*
la acera	*sidewalk, pavement*
la bocacalle	*turning, entrance to a street*
la esquina	*corner*
la manzana	*block (of buildings or houses)*
el paso de peatones	*pedestrian crossing*
el paso de cebra	*pedestrian crossing* Note: literally, 'zebra crossing'
el semáforo	*traffic light*

ESENCIALES

PAGE 139
Directions
1 **B**, **C** 2 **A**, **B**, **C** 3 **D** 4 **B**, **C**
1 **A** 2 **C** 3 **A**, **B** 4 **C**, **D** 5 **D** 6 **A** 7 **C**
1 **B** 2 **A** 3 **C** 4 **B**
1 **B** 2 **A** 3 **A** 4 **B**

....

PAGE 141
Test your vocabulary
1 **D** 2 **B** 3 **C** 4 **C** 5 **A** 6 **C** 7 **A** 8 **C**

....

Degrees of distance
1 **A** 2 **C** 3 **B** 4 **B** 5 **C**
1 **B** 2 **C** 3 **A** 4 **B** 5 **C** 6 **A** 7 **B** 8 **C** 9 **C** 10 **B** 11 **A** 12 **A**

....

PAGE 143
Expressing doubt and certainty
1 **B** 2 **B** 3 **A** 4 **B** 5 **B** 6 **A** 7 **A** 8 **A** 9 **B**
1 **A** 2 **B** 3 **B** 4 **B** 5 **A**

....

PAGE 144
Comprehension and translation
1 **A** 2 **A** 3 **B** 4 **A** 5 **A** 6 **B** 7 **B**

YOUR
SCORE:

Did you get between 0 and 12? ¡Ay, ay, ay!

Did you get between 13 and 25? Muy justito...

Did you get between 26 and 38? No está mal, pero...

Did you get between 39 and 51? Enhorabuena.

Did you get 52 or over? ¡Eres un auténtico fenómeno!

Tema **Driving**

Choose the most suitable option to complete each sentence. More than one may be correct.

Answers page 15

1. ¡Qué coche más ... !

   Ⓐ rápida Ⓑ bonito Ⓒ chulo Ⓓ práctica

2. ... el teórico.

   Ⓐ He aprobado Ⓑ He suspendido Ⓒ He girado Ⓓ He conducido

3. ... el carné.

   Ⓐ Me he saltado Ⓑ He perdido Ⓒ Me he sacado Ⓓ He suspendido

4. ... el semáforo.

   Ⓐ Me he saltado Ⓑ Me he fumado Ⓒ He quemado Ⓓ No he visto

5. El semáforo está en ...

   Ⓐ verde. Ⓑ amarillo. Ⓒ ámbar. Ⓓ rojo.

6. Gasto mucho en ...

   Ⓐ volante. Ⓑ multas. Ⓒ semáforo. Ⓓ inseguridad.

7. Pago ...

   Ⓐ el volante. Ⓑ los atascos. Ⓒ el seguro. Ⓓ la gasolina.

8. Giro ...

   Ⓐ el volante. Ⓑ las multas. Ⓒ el seguro. Ⓓ el atasco.

9. Conduzco ...

   Ⓐ rápido. Ⓑ atasco. Ⓒ retraso. Ⓓ despacio.

Tema **Me too, me neither, I do, I don't**

Based on the following statements, imagine that two people reply: the first has the same opinion and the second has a different opinion. Select the corresponding replies. Example: I like ice cream. / Me too. / I don't.

1. Prefiero desplazarme en bicicleta.
   - (A) Yo sí / Yo tampoco
   - (B) Yo sí / Yo no
   - (C) Yo también / Yo tampoco
   - (D) Yo también / Yo no

Answers page 157

2. Nunca tomo el metro.
   - (A) Yo tampoco / Yo sí
   - (B) Yo no / Yo tampoco
   - (C) Yo tampoco / Yo también
   - (D) Yo no / Yo sí

3. Me molestan los coches.
   - (A) Yo también / Yo no
   - (B) A mí también / A mí no
   - (C) Yo sí / Yo no
   - (D) A mí sí / A mí no

4. No me gustan las vacaciones.
   - (A) Yo no / Yo sí
   - (B) A mí sí / A mí no
   - (C) Yo sí / Yo no
   - (D) A mí tampoco / A mí sí

5. Nunca me salto los semáforos.
   - (A) A mí no / A mí sí
   - (B) Yo tampoco / Yo sí
   - (C) Yo no / Yo tampoco
   - (D) A mí tampoco / A mí sí

Tema **Expressing 'again'**

Select the translation that corresponds to each sentence conveying that something has happened again. More than one may be correct.

Answers page 157

1. There are delays again.
   - (A) Va a haber retrasos.
   - (B) Vuelve a haber retrasos.
   - (C) Puede haber retrasos.

2. I fell down again.
   - (A) Me he podido caer.
   - (B) Me he querido caer.
   - (C) Me he vuelto a caer.

3. Are you driving again?

   Ⓐ ¿Vuelves y conduces?

   Ⓑ ¿Conduces de nuevo?

   Ⓒ ¿Quieres conducir?

4. You failed the driving test again?

   Ⓐ ¿Has suspendido otra vez el práctico?

   Ⓑ ¿Has vuelto suspendiendo el práctico?

   Ⓒ ¿Has querido suspender el práctico?

5. Are you going to retake the driving test?

   Ⓐ ¿Vas a pasar otra vez el práctico?

   Ⓑ ¿Vas a pasar de nuevo el práctico?

   Ⓒ ¿Vas a volver a pasar el práctico?

Tema Don't!

Select the corresponding prohibition for each command.

Answers page 157

1. ¡Gira a la izquierda!

   Ⓐ No gires a la izquierda.
   Ⓑ No giras a la izquierda.
   Ⓒ No gira a la izquierda.

2. ¡Bebe!

   Ⓐ No bebes.
   Ⓑ No bebáis.
   Ⓒ No bebas.

3. ¡Escríbeme!

   Ⓐ No me escribís.
   Ⓑ No me escribas.
   Ⓒ No me escribes.

4. ¡Créelo!

   Ⓐ No lo craes.
   Ⓑ No lo creas.
   Ⓒ No lo crees.

5. ¡Hablad!

   Ⓐ No hables.
   Ⓑ No habléis.
   Ⓒ No hablas.

6. ¡Conducid rápido!

   Ⓐ No conducid rápido.
   Ⓑ No conduzáis rápido.
   Ⓒ No conduzcáis rápido.

7. ¡Levántate!

    Ⓐ No te levantas.   Ⓑ No te levantes.   Ⓒ No levántate.

8. ¡Dime algo!

    Ⓐ No dimes nada.   Ⓑ No me dices nada.   Ⓒ No me digas nada.

Tema **Expressing disagreement**

Select the correct way to disagree with each opinion.

1. El metro es peligroso.

    Ⓐ No pienso que el metro es peligroso.

    Ⓑ No pienso que el metro sea peligroso.

    Ⓒ No pienso que el metro está peligroso.

Answers page 157

2. Estás hecho para conducir.

    Ⓐ No creo que estés hecho para conducir.

    Ⓑ No creo que seas hecho para conducir.

    Ⓒ No creo que estás hecho para conducir.

3. Tenéis razón.

    Ⓐ No estoy seguro de que tenáis razón.

    Ⓑ No estoy seguro de que tengáis razón.

    Ⓒ No estoy seguro de que tiengáis razón.

4. Nos gusta este coche.

    Ⓐ No estamos convencidos de que nos guste este coche.

    Ⓑ No estamos convencidos de que nos gustemos este coche.

    Ⓒ No estamos convencidos de que nos gusta este coche.

5. Vivimos más felices sin coche.

    Ⓐ No es verdad que vivemos más felices sin coche.

    Ⓑ No es verdad que vivamos más felices sin coche.

    Ⓒ No es verdad que vivimos más felices sin coche.

Unit 16
ESENCIALES

Choose the correct form of the verb to complete each statement.

Answers page 157

1. Me gusta que la gente ... en bicicleta.

   Ⓐ va   Ⓑ ve   Ⓒ vaya

2. Me parece bien que ... una tortilla.

   Ⓐ haces   Ⓑ hayas   Ⓒ hagas

3. A mi perro le encanta que ... a su lado.

   Ⓐ me siente   Ⓑ me sienta   Ⓒ me siento

4. A mis padres les da igual que ... tarde a casa.

   Ⓐ vuelva   Ⓑ vuelve   Ⓒ vuelvo

5. Me horroriza que ... tan imprudentes.

   Ⓐ sois   Ⓑ seáis   Ⓒ estéis

Tema *Hasta que* (until) or *aunque* (even though)?

Select the most appropriate option for each context.

1. Voy a sacarme el carné...

   Ⓐ hasta que lo quieras.   Ⓑ aunque no lo quieras.

Answers page 157

2. Voy a insistir...

   Ⓐ hasta que lo saque.   Ⓑ aunque lo saque.

3. Voy a tomar clases...

   Ⓐ hasta que lo apruebe.   Ⓑ aunque lo apruebe.

4. Voy a pedirte el coche...

   Ⓐ hasta que me digas que sí.   Ⓑ aunque me digas que sí.

5. Conduzco muy bien...

   Ⓐ hasta que pienses lo contrario.   Ⓑ aunque pienses lo contrario.

6. Voy a conseguir el carné...

   Ⓐ hasta que suspenda veinte veces.   Ⓑ aunque suspenda veinte veces.

Tema Making comparisons

Choose the appropriate phrase in each case.

Answers
page 157

1. Un coche es ... una bicicleta.

   (A) más rápido que   (B) menos rápido que

2. Londres está ... que Moscú.

   (A) más lejos de París   (B) menos lejos de París

3. La Luna está ... que el Sol.

   (A) más cerca de la Tierra (B) menos cerca de la Tierra

4. El barco es ... el avión.

   (A) más lento que   (B) menos lento que

5. Andar es ... tomar el coche.

   (A) más ecológico que   (B) menos ecológico que

6. El metro es ... el tren.

   (A) más caro que   (B) menos caro que

Select the correct form of 'as (much/many)' to complete each sentence.

Answers
page 157

1. Soy ... nerviosa como tú.

   (A) tan   (B) tanto   (C) tantos

   (D) tanta   (E) tantas

2. No sois ... prácticos como yo.

   (A) tan   (B) tanto   (C) tantos

   (D) tanta   (E) tantas

3. Me mareo ... en el tren como el barco.

   (A) tan   (B) tanto   (C) tantos

   (D) tanta   (E) tantas

4. Las multas me cuestan ... como la gasolina.

   (A) tan   (B) tanto   (C) tantos

   (D) tanta   (E) tantas

5. No le tengo ... miedo al avión como tú.

A tan
B tanto
C tantos
D tanta
E tantas

6. No he suspendido el carné ... veces como tú.

A tan
B tanto
C tantos
D tanta
E tantas

7. No hay ... coches a mediodía como por la tarde.

A tan
B tanto
C tantos
D tanta
E tantas

8. No hay ... gente como crees.

A tan
B tanto
C tantos
D tanta
E tantas

Tema **Comprehension and translation**

Select the equivalent translation for each sentence.

Answers page 157

1. I go everywhere by bicycle.

A Voy en todas partes a bicicleta.

B Voy a todas partes en bicicleta.

C Voy todas partes por bicicleta.

2. I feel at home everywhere.

A Me siento en casa a todas partes.

B Me siento a casa a todas partes.

C Me siento en casa en todas partes.

3. In Madrid, people are just about everywhere.

A A Madrid, la gente es un poco de todas partes.

B En Madrid, la gente es un poco de todas partes.

C En Madrid, la gente está un poco por todas partes.

4. Le tengo miedo a los transportes colectivos.

   Ⓐ I'm not a big fan of public transport.

   Ⓑ I have problems with public transport.

   Ⓒ I'm afraid of public transport.

5. Me trae cuenta coger un taxi.

   Ⓐ It makes sense for me to get a taxi.

   Ⓑ I just realized that I need to get a taxi.

   Ⓒ I count on getting a taxi.

Verbs

ÚTILES

conducir	*to drive*
desplazarse	*to move around, to get about*
fumar	*to smoke* Note: **fumarse una clase** *to skip class*, **fumarse un semáforo** *to run a red light*
insistir	*to insist, to persevere*
marearse	*to get motion sickness, to feel nauseous*
molestar	*to bother, to disturb*
sacar	*to take out* Note: **sacarse** *to receive* (e.g. a diploma, certificate, etc.)
saltar	*to jump* Note: **saltarse** means the same thing as **fumarse**.

Expressions

tenerle miedo a	*to be afraid of* (**Le tengo miedo a ...** *I'm scared of ...*)
traer cuenta	*to be convenient, to make sense, to be worthwhile* (**Me trae cuenta** + infinitive *It makes sense for me* + infinitive)
volver a + infinitive	*expresses a repeated action* (**Vuelvo a salir** *I'm going back out*). Other expressions to convey this include **de nuevo** or **otra vez** *again*.

Transport and driving

el avión	*airplane*
el barco	*ship, boat*
la bicicleta	*bicycle*
el coche	*car*
el metro	*metro*
el tren	*train*
el carné	*driving permit*
el práctico	*driving test*
el teórico	*written driving test*
la gasolina	*petrol, gasoline*
la multa	*fine*
el seguro	*insurance*
el volante	*steering wheel*
ámbar	*yellow, amber* (traffic light)
el atasco	*traffic jam*
despacio	*slowly*
imprudente	*reckless*
la inseguridad	*insecurity*
nervioso/a	*nervous* (m./f.)
peligroso/a	*dangerous* (m./f.)
rápido/a	*rapid* (m./f.)
el retraso	*delay*

Subordinating conjunctions

hasta que	*until*
aunque	*even if, although*

ESENCIALES

PAGE 148
Driving
1 **B**, **C**   2 **A**, **B**   3 **B**, **C**, **D**   4 **A**, **B**, **C**   5 **A**, **C**, **D**   6 **B**   7 **C**, **D**   8 **A**   9 **A**, **D**

Me too, me neither, I do, I don't
1 **D**   2 **A**   3 **B**   4 **D**   5 **B**

PAGE 149
Expressing 'again'
1 **B**   2 **C**   3 **B**   4 **A**   5 **A**, **B**, **C**

PAGE 150
Don't!
1 **A**   2 **C**   3 **B**   4 **B**   5 **B**   6 **C**   7 **B**   8 **C**

PAGE 151
Expressing disagreement
1 **B**   2 **A**   3 **B**   4 **A**   5 **B**

PAGE 152
Conveying degrees of appreciation
1 **C**   2 **C**   3 **A**   4 **A**   5 **B**

Hasta que (until) or *aunque* (even though)?
1 **B**   2 **A**   3 **A**   4 **A**   5 **B**   6 **B**

PAGE 153
Making comparisons
1 **A**   2 **B**   3 **A**   4 **A**   5 **A**   6 **B**
1 **A**   2 **A**   3 **B**   4 **B**   5 **B**   6 **E**   7 **C**   8 **D**

PAGE 154
Comprehension and translation
1 **B**   2 **C**   3 **B**   4 **C**   5 **A**

Did you get between 0 and 12? ¡Ay, ay, ay!

Did you get between 13 and 25? Muy justito...

Did you get between 26 and 38? No está mal, pero...

Did you get between 39 and 51? Enhorabuena.

Did you get 52 or over? ¡Eres un auténtico fenómeno!

YOUR SCORE:

Unit 17
ESENCIALES

Tema **Money and banks**

Select the correct verb phrase to complete each sentence.

Answers page 166

1. ¿... con tarjeta o en efectivo?

   Ⓐ Se ha tragado   Ⓒ Me permite

   Ⓑ No se aceptan   Ⓓ Va a pagar

2. El cajero ... mi tarjeta de crédito.

   Ⓐ se ha tragado   Ⓒ me permite

   Ⓑ no se aceptan   Ⓓ va a pagar

3. ¿... su DNI, por favor?

   Ⓐ Se ha tragado   Ⓒ Me permite

   Ⓑ No se aceptan   Ⓓ Va a pagar

4. ... talones, lo siento.

   Ⓐ Se ha tragado   Ⓒ Me permite

   Ⓑ No se aceptan   Ⓓ Va a pagar

Choose the most suitable phrase in each case.

Answers page 166

1. Quiero hacer ...

   Ⓐ un reintegro.   Ⓒ dinero de mi cuenta.

   Ⓑ mal el pin.   Ⓓ una sucursal del banco.

2. He tecleado...

   Ⓐ un reintegro.   Ⓒ dinero de mi cuenta.

   Ⓑ mal el pin.   Ⓓ una sucursal del banco.

3. ¿Dónde hay ...?

   Ⓐ un reintegro   Ⓒ dinero de mi cuenta

   Ⓑ mal el pin   Ⓓ una sucursal del banco

4. Tengo que sacar...

   Ⓐ un reintegro.   Ⓒ dinero de mi cuenta.

   Ⓑ mal el pin.   Ⓓ una sucursal del banco.

| Tema | **Expressions with religious roots** |

Select the current meaning of each expression.

Answers page 166

1. No hay Dios que duerma.

   Ⓐ It's not possible to sleep.   Ⓑ God sees everything.

2. No hay ni Dios.

   Ⓐ There is no one around.   Ⓑ You can't see anything.

3. Estás hecho un Cristo.

   Ⓐ You're looking really well.   Ⓑ You're looking terrible.

4. Lo sabe todo Cristo.

   Ⓐ Everyone knows it.   Ⓑ Only God knows it.

5. No estoy muy católico.

   Ⓐ I'm not feeling very well.   Ⓑ I don't believe in God.

6. Tengo el santo de espaldas.

   Ⓐ I have no luck.   Ⓑ I'm not scared of anything.

7. Tengo el santo de cara.

   Ⓐ I'm lucky.   Ⓑ I better be careful.

8. Vaya por Dios.

   Ⓐ God is my shepherd.   Ⓑ For goodness sake.

| Tema | **To become, get, turn + adj.: *ponerse* or *volverse*?** |

Choose the correct verb phrase conveying transformation in each context.

1. ... enfermo.

   Ⓐ Te vas a volver   Ⓑ Te vas a poner

Answers page 166

2. Con la edad la gente ... torpe.

   Ⓐ se pone   Ⓑ se vuelve

3. Algunas personas ... nervioso.

   Ⓐ me ponen   Ⓑ me vuelven

4. De noche ... triste.

   Ⓐ me pongo

   Ⓑ me vuelvo

5. Te ... muy gordo en unas semanas.

   Ⓐ has puesto

   Ⓑ has vuelto

6. El pobre se ... loco.

   Ⓐ ha puesto

   Ⓑ ha vuelto

7. ¡Vaya coche! ¿Te ... rico?

   Ⓐ has puesto

   Ⓑ has vuelto

8. ¿Por qué te ... tan contento?

   Ⓐ has puesto

   Ⓑ has vuelto

Tema Commands

*Select the **tratamiento** (form of address) used in each command.*

Answers
page 166

1. Permíteme el pasaporte, por favor.

   Ⓐ Informal

   Ⓑ Formal

2. Déjame el DNI.

   Ⓐ Informal

   Ⓑ Formal

3. Devuélvame la tarjeta de crédito.

   Ⓐ Informal

   Ⓑ Formal

4. Espéreme cerca del banco.

   Ⓐ Informal

   Ⓑ Formal

5. Ayúdeme, por favor.

   Ⓐ Informal

   Ⓑ Formal

6. ¡Olvídame!

   Ⓐ Informal

   Ⓑ Formal

7. ¡Págueme!

   Ⓐ Informal

   Ⓑ Formal

8. Sácame cien euros del cajero.

    Ⓐ Informal   Ⓑ Formal

Tema   **Exclamations**

Select the exclamation that corresponds to each sentence.

**Answers
page 166**

1. Los jóvenes son torpes.

    Ⓐ ¡Qué torpes son los jóvenes!

    Ⓑ ¡Qué torpes los jóvenes son!

2. El personal de la sucursal es amable.

    Ⓐ ¡Qué amable es el personal de la sucursal!

    Ⓑ ¡Qué más amable es el personal de la sucursal!

3. El padre de Juan se ha puesto muy viejo.

    Ⓐ ¡Qué se ha puesto viejo el padre de Juan!

    Ⓑ ¡Qué viejo se ha puesto el padre de Juan!

4. Mi sobrino se levanta muy tarde.

    Ⓐ ¡Qué tarde se levanta mi sobrino!

    Ⓑ ¡Qué tarde mi sobrino se levanta!

5. Usted tiene un abuelo muy despistado.

    Ⓐ ¡Qué más despistado abuelo usted tiene!

    Ⓑ ¡Qué abuelo más despistado tiene usted!

Tema   *Haber* (auxiliary verb) or *hacer*?

Select the correct verb to complete each sentence.

**Answers
page 166**

1. No pienso que ... mucha gente en el banco.

    Ⓐ haga   Ⓑ haya

2. Quizás se ... vuelto locos.

    Ⓐ hagan   Ⓑ hayan

3. No creo que ... mucho tiempo que trabaja en ese banco.

 A) haga
 B) haya

4. Es tarde, no pienso que ... tiempo para ir al banco hoy.

 A) haga
 B) haya

5. Tal vez ... comida en el frigorífico, no sé.

 A) haga
 B) haya

6. No creo que ... tecleado mal el pin.

 A) hagamos
 B) hayamos

7. ¿Te da igual que ... perdido la tarjeta?

 A) haga
 B) haya

8. Os pido que hoy ... la compra vosotros.

 A) hagáis
 B) hayáis

Tema | **Irregular verbs ending in *-gar* and *-car***

Choose the correct ending for the verb in each sentence.

Answers page 166

1. Quiero que sa... cien euros del cajero.

 A) ...cas
 B) ...quas
 C) ...ces
 D) ...ques

2. ¿Me sa... cien euros, por favor?

 A) ...cas
 B) ...quas
 C) ...ces
 D) ...ques

3. Si tecleas mal el pin, el cajero se tra... tu tarjeta.

 A) ...ga
 B) ...gua
 C) ...ge
 D) ...gue

4. Si tecleas mal el pin, puede que el cajero se tra... tu tarjeta.

 A) ...ga
 B) ...gua
 C) ...ge
 D) ...gue

5. Me pone muy nervioso que siempre te equivo... de pin.

 A) ...cas
 B) ...quas
 C) ...ces
 D) ...ques

6. ¿Por qué te equivo... siempre de pin?

 A) ...cas
 B) ...quas
 C) ...ces
 D) ...ques

7. Esta vez no quiero que pa... vosotros.

Ⓐ ...gáis   Ⓑ ...quáis   Ⓒ ...géis   Ⓓ ...guéis

8. ¿Pa... vosotros?

Ⓐ ...gáis   Ⓑ ...quáis   Ⓒ ...géis   Ⓓ ...guéis

Tema *Quedar or quedarse?*

Choose the correct verb for each context.

Answers page 166

1. ¿Por dónde ... la sucursal del banco?

Ⓐ se queda   Ⓑ queda

2. ¿... dinero para hacer la compra?

Ⓐ Se queda   Ⓑ Queda

3. ¿... en casa este fin de semana o salís?

Ⓐ Os quedáis   Ⓑ Quedáis

4. Pagas el alquiler, los recibos y ... sin un duro.

Ⓐ te quedas   Ⓑ quedas

5. ¿... mi tarjeta o me la devuelven?

Ⓐ Se quedan con   Ⓑ Quedan con

6. ¿... para ir de copas?

Ⓐ Nos quedamos   Ⓑ Quedamos

7. ¿A qué hora ... con ellos?

Ⓐ te has quedado   Ⓑ has quedado

8. ¿Te vas de vacaciones o ... en Madrid?

Ⓐ te quedas   Ⓑ quedas

9. Creo que ese restaurante ... bastante lejos.

Ⓐ se queda   Ⓑ queda

10. ¿Vienes o ... aquí?

Ⓐ te quedas   Ⓑ quedas

| **Tema** | **Comprehension and translation** |

Select the option with the same meaning in each case.

Answers
page 166

1. Basta con ir al mostrador para hacer un reintegro.

   A I'm fed up with going to the machine to make a withdrawal.

   B Just go to the counter and make a withdrawal.

2. ¿Pagar con cheque? ¡Qué más quisiera!

   A Pay by cheque? What more could I want!

   B Pay by cheque? Who would want to do that!

3. Le atiendo ahora mismo.

   A I'll be with you right away.

   B I'm waiting for him right here.

4. Shall we meet up tomorrow?

   A ¿Quedamos mañana?

   B ¿Quedamos por la mañana?

5. Shall we meet up tomorrow morning?

   A ¿Quedamos mañana mañana?

   B ¿Quedamos mañana por la mañana?

| **Verbs** | ÚTILES |

aceptar	*to accept*
bastar	*to be enough* (**basta con** *it suffices to, just* + verb)
devolver	*to return, to take back* Note: verb with a spelling change
equivocarse	*to be wrong, to be mistaken*
olvidar	*to forget*
permitir	*to permit, to allow, may I …?*
ponerse	*to become, to get* (used like **estar**: to express transitory states such as moods, health, etc.)

quedar	*to remain (to be left), to be located, to arrange to meet, to meet*
quedarse	*to stay (somewhere), to find oneself (in a situation)* (**quedarse con** *to keep, to take*)
sacar	*to withdraw (money)*
teclear	*to key in, to enter (on a keyboard)*
tragar	*to swallow*
volverse	*to become, to get* (used like **ser**: lasting states, traits, characteristics, etc.) Note: verb with a spelling change

At the bank

el banco	*bank*
el cajero	*cash machine, ATM*
el cheque	*cheque*
la cuenta	*account*
el DNI	*ID, identity card*
en efectivo	*in cash*
el mostrador	*counter*
el pasaporte	*passport*
el pin	*PIN (personal identification number)*
el reintegro	*withdrawal, refund*
la sucursal	*branch office*
el talón	*cheque*
la tarjeta	*card*

Adjectives

enfermo/a	*sick, ill* (m./f.)
nervioso/a	*nervous* (m./f.)
torpe	*clumsy, awkward*

165

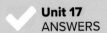

Unit 17
ANSWERS

ESENCIALES

PAGE 158
Money and banks
1 **D** 2 **A** 3 **C** 4 **B**
1 **A** 2 **B** 3 **D** 4 **C**

PAGE 159
Expressions with religious roots
1 **A** 2 **A** 3 **B** 4 **A** 5 **A** 6 **A** 7 **A** 8 **B**

To become, get, turn + adj.: *ponerse* or *volverse*?
1 **B** 2 **B** 3 **A** 4 **A** 5 **A** 6 **B** 7 **B** 8 **A**

PAGE 160
Commands
1 **A** 2 **A** 3 **B** 4 **B** 5 **B** 6 **A** 7 **B** 8 **A**

PAGE 161
Exclamations
1 **A** 2 **A** 3 **B** 4 **A** 5 **B**

Haber (auxiliary verb) or *hacer*?
1 **B** 2 **B** 3 **A** 4 **B** 5 **B** 6 **B** 7 **B** 8 **A**

PAGE 162
Irregular verbs ending in *-gar* and *-car*
1 **D** 2 **A** 3 **A** 4 **D** 5 **D** 6 **A** 7 **D** 8 **A**

PAGE 163
Quedar or *quedarse*?
1 **B** 2 **B** 3 **A** 4 **A** 5 **A** 6 **B** 7 **B** 8 **A** 9 **B** 10 **A**

PAGE 164
Comprehension and translation
1 **B** 2 **A** 3 **A** 4 **A** 5 **B**

YOUR
SCORE:

Did you get between 0 and 14? **¡Ay, ay, ay!**

Did you get between 15 and 28? **Muy justito...**

Did you get between 29 and 42? **No está mal, pero...**

Did you get between 43 and 56? **Enhorabuena.**

Did you get 57 or over? **¡Eres un auténtico fenómeno!**

Tema Letters and post

Choose the most suitable option to complete each sentence. More than one answer may be correct.

Answers page 175

1. Tengo que escribir ... a mi abuela.

   A una letra   B un mapa   C una carta

2. ¿Cuánto cuesta ... para Francia?

   A un sello   B un timbre   C un timbro

3. ¡Qué ... más bonita!

   A postal   B tarjeta postal   C carta postal

4. Necesito ...

   A un sobre.   B una sobre.   C una sobra.

5. Voy a echar una carta ...

   A al buzón.   B a Correos.   C al estanco.

6. Me gusta escribir con ...

   A estylo.   B pluma.   C bolígrafo.

7. Préstame ..., por favor.

   A una hoja de papel   B un papiro   C un folio

Tema Internet and email

Select the Spanish term that corresponds to each word related to digital technology. More than one answer may be correct.

Answers page 175

1. @ ('at')

   A arobase   B aroba   C arroba

2. dot

   A punto   B punta   C punti

3. dash

   A tira   B línea   C guion

4. slash
   - (A) barra
   - (B) cruz
   - (C) raya

5. message
   - (A) mesaje
   - (B) mensaje
   - (C) masaje

6. to download
   - (A) descargar
   - (B) bajarse
   - (C) telecargarse

7. to upload
   - (A) subir
   - (B) alinear
   - (C) recargar

Tema **Cardinal and ordinal numbers**

Select the correct ending for each sentence.

Answers
page 175

1. En 1807, Beethoven compone...
   - (A) la quinta sinfonía.
   - (B) la sinfonía cinco.
   - (C) la cinco sinfonía.

2. El fuego es el ...
   - (A) cuarto elemento.
   - (B) cuatro elemento.
   - (C) elemento cuarto.

3. El rey de España es...
   - (A) Felipe seis.
   - (B) Felipe sexto.
   - (C) Felipe el seis.

4. El padre de Felipe VI se llama...
   - (A) Juan Carlos uno.
   - (B) Juan Carlos primer.
   - (C) Juan Carlos primero.

5. El abuelo de Felipe VI se llamó...
   - (A) Alfonso decimotercero.
   - (B) Alfonso trece.
   - (C) Alfonso decimotercer.

6. Yo nací en el ...
   - (A) veinte siglo.
   - (B) siglo veinte.
   - (C) vigésimo siglo.

7. Los dos últimos papas han sido...
   - (A) Juan Pablo segundo y Benedicto decimosexto.
   - (B) Juan Pablo segundo y Benedicto dieciséis.
   - (C) Juan Pablo dos y Benedicto decimosexto.

Tema | Some expressions with reflexive verbs

Using the elements provided, select the correct construction of the Spanish phrase in the present perfect.

1. tú / borrarse / todos los mensajes

   Ⓐ Se te has borrado todos los mensajes.

   Ⓑ Se te han borrado todos los mensajes.

   Ⓒ Se te ha borrado todos los mensajes.

   Answers page 175

2. vosotros / estropearse / el móvil

   Ⓐ Se os ha estropeado el móvil.

   Ⓑ Se os habéis estropeado el móvil.

   Ⓒ Se os han estropeado el móvil.

3. nosotros / caerse / el pelo

   Ⓐ Se nos hemos caído el pelo.

   Ⓑ Se nos han caído el pelo.

   Ⓒ Se nos ha caído el pelo.

4. yo / perderse / las llaves

   Ⓐ Se me he perdido las llaves.

   Ⓑ Se me han perdido las llaves.

   Ⓒ Se me ha perdido las llaves.

5. ellas / olvidarse / el DNI

   Ⓐ Se les han olvidado el DNI.

   Ⓑ Se le han olvidado el DNI.

   Ⓒ Se les ha olvidado el DNI.

6. usted / romperse / las gafas

   Ⓐ Se le han roto las gafas.

   Ⓑ Se les ha roto las gafas.

   Ⓒ Se les han roto las gafas.

Unit 18
ESENCIALES

Tema Commands

*Select the command in the second-person singular (**tú**) that corresponds to each of these commands in the second-person plural (**vosotros**).*

1. Haced vuestro trabajo.

   A Hace tu trabajo. B Haze tu trabajo. C Haz tu trabajo.

2. Poned la mesa.

   A Pon la mesa. B Pone la mesa. C Pones la mesa.

3. Tened amigos.

   A Tien amigos. B Ten amigos. C Tene amigos.

4. Salid a pasear.

   A Sal a pasear. B Sale a pasear. C Sales a pasear.

*Now select the command in the second-person plural (**vosotros**) that corresponds to each of these commands in the second-person singular (**tú**).*

1. Ven a visitarme.

   A Vened a visitarme. B Vienid a visitarme. C Venid a visitarme.

2. Dime la verdad.

   A Decidme la verdad. B Dicidme la verdad. C Dicedme la verdad.

3. Sé bueno.

   A Seíd buenos. B Sied buenos. C Sed buenos.

4. Ve a hacer la compra.

   A Vad a hacer la compra. B Id a hacer la compra. C Ved a hacer la compra.

Tema Conjugation: *reír* and *sonreír*

Choose the correct form of the verb for each context.

1. ¿De qué te ... ?

   A rees B ríes C ris

2. De nada, me ... solo.

   Ⓐ reo   Ⓑ reio   Ⓒ río

3. Siempre nos ... mucho contigo.

   Ⓐ reímos   Ⓑ reemos   Ⓒ ríemos

4. Y vosotros, ¿por qué me ... ?

   Ⓐ sonríeis   Ⓑ sonrís   Ⓒ sonreís

5. La gente nunca ... con mis chistes.

   Ⓐ ree   Ⓑ ríe   Ⓒ ri

6. Si mis padres te ..., es que les caes bien.

   Ⓐ sonríen   Ⓑ sonreen   Ⓒ sonreín

7. Siempre están ...

   Ⓐ reyendo.   Ⓑ reíndo.   Ⓒ riendo.

8. En una entrevista de trabajo, ... siempre.

   Ⓐ sonreie   Ⓑ sonríe   Ⓒ sonre

9. Para ser felices, ... a la vida.

   Ⓐ sonreíd   Ⓑ sonríed   Ⓒ sonrid

Tema **Conversing and joking**

Put the conversation in the most logical order.

1. A. Bueno, no es para tanto.

   B. Qué lástima, se me han perdido 5 euros.

   C. Vale, pero no tiene ninguna gracia.

Answers page 175

   Ⓐ A – C – B   Ⓑ C – A – B   Ⓒ B – A – C

2. A. Cuéntamelo, me suelen hacer gracia.

   B. Es buenísimo, escucha.

   C. ¿Conoces el último chiste del panadero?

   Ⓐ A – C – B   Ⓑ C – A – B   Ⓒ B – A – C

3. A. Me encantan las bromas del panadero.

   B. A mí sí me hacen reir.

   C. Pues no tienen gracia.

   Ⓐ A – C – B   Ⓑ C – A – B   Ⓒ B – A – C

Tema Fortunately / unfortunately

Select the appropriate response to each question.

Answers
page 175

1. ¿A ti se te han borrado fotos alguna vez?
   Ⓐ Sí, por suerte.   Ⓑ Sí, desgraciadamente.

2. ¿Te encuentras mal?
   Ⓐ Sí, por suerte.   Ⓑ Sí, desgraciadamente.

3. ¿Hay algún hospital cerca de aquí?
   Ⓐ Sí, por suerte.   Ⓑ Sí, desgraciadamente.

4. ¿Es verdad que se te ha muerto el perro?
   Ⓐ Sí, por suerte.   Ⓑ Sí, desgraciadamente.

5. Tengo que echar una carta. ¿Está abierto Correos?
   Ⓐ Sí, por suerte.   Ⓑ Sí, desgraciadamente.

6. ¿Se puede arreglar mi móvil?
   Ⓐ Sí, por suerte.   Ⓑ Sí, desgraciadamente.

Tema *Dejar* (to leave) or *quitar* (to take away)?

Select the most appropriate verb in each case.

Answers
page 175

1. No me ..., por favor.
   Ⓐ dejes   Ⓑ quites

2. Si me ..., me muero.
   Ⓐ dejas   Ⓑ quitas

3. Si me ... el móvil, me muero.
   Ⓐ dejas   Ⓑ quitas

4. Si sigues tan adicto al móvil, te lo voy a ...

    (A) dejar.   (B) quitar.

5. Te ... el móvil, pero solo para que me llames, ¿vale?

    (A) dejo   (B) quito

6. Vamos a cenar : ... el móvil de la mesa.

    (A) deja   (B) quita

Verbs and expressions

ÚTILES

arreglar	*to repair, to sort out, to resolve*
borrar	*to erase, to delete*
dejar	*to leave*
echar (una carta)	*to send a letter*
encontrarse	*to meet* Note: verb with a spelling change
estropear	*to destroy, to damage*
morir / morirse	*to die* Note: verb with a spelling change
quitar	*to take away, to take off*
reír	*to laugh* Note: verb with a spelling change
romper	*to break* Note: irregular past participle: **roto**
sonreír	*to smile* Note: verb with a spelling change
dar lástima / dar pena	*to sadden, to make sad*
hacer gracia a alguno	*to find funny or amusing*
tener gracia	*to be funny or amusing*

Ordinal numbers Only the first ten ordinal numbers are commonly used in Spanish.

primero/a	*first* (m./f.)
segundo/a	*second* (m./f.)
tercero/a	*third* (m./f.)
cuarto/a	*fourth* (m./f.)

quinto/a	*fifth* (m./f.)
sexto/a	*sixth* (m./f.)
séptimo/a	*seventh* (m./f.)
octavo/a	*eighth* (m./f.)
noveno/a	*ninth* (m./f.)
décimo/a	*tenth* (m./f.)

Letters and the post

el bolígrafo	*ballpoint pen*
el buzón	*letterbox, postbox, mailbox*
la carta	*letter*
el correo	*post, mail (**correos** post office)*
el estanco	*tobacconist's*
el folio	*sheet of paper*
la hoja	*leaf, page of a document*
el papel	*paper*
la pluma	*fountain pen*
la postal	*postcard*
el sello	*stamp*
el sobre	*envelope*
la tarjeta	*card*

Useful phrases

desgraciadamente	*unfortunately*
por suerte	*fortunately, luckily*
no es para tanto	*it's no big deal, it's not that bad*

ESENCIALES

PAGE 167
Letters and post
1 **C** 2 **A** 3 **A, B** 4 **A** 5 **A, B** 6 **B, C** 7 **A, C**

Internet and email
1 **C** 2 **A** 3 **C** 4 **A** 5 **B** 6 **A, B** 7 **A**

PAGE 168
Cardinal and ordinal numbers
1 **A** 2 **A** 3 **B** 4 **C** 5 **B** 6 **B** 7 **B**

PAGE 169
Some expressions with reflexive verbs
1 **B** 2 **A** 3 **C** 4 **B** 5 **C** 6 **A**

PAGE 170
Commands
1 **C** 2 **A** 3 **B** 4 **A**
1 **C** 2 **A** 3 **C** 4 **B**

Conjugation: *reír* and **sonreír**
1 **B** 2 **C** 3 **A** 4 **C** 5 **B** 6 **A** 7 **C** 8 **B** 9 **A**

PAGE 171
Conversing and joking
1 **C** 2 **B** 3 **A**

PAGE 172
Fortunately / unfortunately
1 **B** 2 **B** 3 **A** 4 **B** 5 **A** 6 **A**

Dejar (to leave) or *quitar* (to take away)?
1 **A** 2 **A** 3 **B** 4 **B** 5 **A** 6 **B**

YOUR
SCORE:

Did you get between 0 and 11? ¡Ay, ay, ay!

Did you get between 12 and 23? Muy justito...

Did you get between 24 and 35? No está mal, pero...

Did you get between 36 and 47? Enhorabuena.

Did you get 48 or over? ¡Eres un auténtico fenómeno!

| Tema | **Pronunciation and spelling: ü** |

Select the correct spelling of the Spanish term. The phonetic transcriptions are provided in brackets.

Answers page 185

1. [ghee-tar-rah]
   - A guitarra
   - B güitarra

2. [bee-leen-gway]
   - A bilingue
   - B bilingüe

3. [gayr-rah]
   - A guerra
   - B güerra

4. [see-gway-nyah]
   - A cigueña
   - B cigüeña

5. [an-tee-gwoh]
   - A antiguo
   - B antigüo

6. [ee-gwah-nah]
   - A iguana
   - B igüana

7. [vayr-gwen-thah]
   - A verguenza
   - B vergüenza

8. [am-bee-gwoh]
   - A ambiguo
   - B ambigüo

9. [par-ah-gwahs]
   - A paraguas
   - B paragüas

10. [peen-gwee-noh]
    - A pinguino
    - B pingüino

| Tema | **Written accents** |

Select the correct spelling of the word in each case, with or without an accent.

1. Dime ... piensas de eso.
   - A que
   - B qué

Answers page 185

2. No es posible, dime … no es verdad.

   Ⓐ que   Ⓑ qué

3. Imagina … vamos de viaje al Caribe.

   Ⓐ que   Ⓑ qué

4. ¡Imagina … ha ocurrido en la panadería!

   Ⓐ que   Ⓑ qué

5. ¿Sabes … me han robado la cartera?

   Ⓐ que   Ⓑ qué

6. ¿Sabes … tengo para ti?

   Ⓐ que   Ⓑ qué

7. ¿Puede decir … es esa persona?

   Ⓐ como   Ⓑ cómo

8. Las cosas no son … tú piensas.

   Ⓐ como   Ⓑ cómo

9. Me encanta la ciudad … vivo.

   Ⓐ donde   Ⓑ dónde

10. Me pregunto … está viviendo ahora.

   Ⓐ donde   Ⓑ dónde

Tema | **Containers and contents**

Choose the most suitable object for each context.

Answers page 185

1. Llevo la agenda en…

   Ⓐ el bolso.   Ⓒ el bolsillo.

   Ⓑ la bolsa.   Ⓓ la cartera.

2. Llevo el dinero en …

   Ⓐ el bolso.   Ⓒ el bolsillo.

   Ⓑ la bolsa.   Ⓓ la cartera.

3. Pongo la compra en...

Ⓐ el bolso.

Ⓒ el bolsillo.

Ⓑ la bolsa.

Ⓓ la cartera.

4. Meto la mano en...

Ⓐ el bolso.

Ⓒ el bolsillo.

Ⓑ la bolsa.

Ⓓ la cartera.

Tema Commands

Select the formal equivalent of each of these informal commands.

Answers page 185

1. Siéntate.

Ⓐ Siéntese.

Ⓑ Siéntase.

Ⓒ Síntase.

2. Cuéntame.

Ⓐ Cóntame.

Ⓑ Cónteme.

Ⓒ Cuénteme.

3. Cállate.

Ⓐ Cállese.

Ⓑ Cállase.

Ⓒ Cállete.

4. Devuélveme la cartera.

Ⓐ Devólvame la cartera.

Ⓑ Devólveme la cartera.

Ⓒ Devuélvame la cartera.

5. Levantaos.

Ⓐ Levántase.

Ⓑ Levántesen.

Ⓒ Levántense.

6. Poneos gafas de sol.

Ⓐ Pónganse gafas de sol.

Ⓑ Póngasen gafas de sol.

Ⓒ Póngansen gafas de sol.

7. Despertaos.

Ⓐ Despiértesen.

Ⓑ Despértense.

Ⓒ Despiértense.

8. Servíos.

Ⓐ Sírvanse.

Ⓑ Sérvanse.

Ⓒ Sérvense.

Tema The imperfect

Select the correct sentence in the imperfect tense.

Answers page 185

1. El ladrón lleva el pelo largo.
   - A El ladrón llevía el pelo largo.
   - B El ladrón llevaba el pelo largo.

2. ¿Dónde os encontráis?
   - A ¿Dónde os encontrabais?
   - B ¿Dónde os encontríais?

3. Volvemos tranquilamente a casa.
   - A Volvíamos tranquilamente a casa.
   - B Volvébamos tranquilamente a casa.

4. Andamos despacio.
   - A Andíamos despacio.
   - B Andábamos despacio.

5. Unos hombres piden dinero.
   - A Unos hombres pediban dinero.
   - B Unos hombres pedían dinero.

6. Tengo mucho miedo.
   - A Tienía mucho miedo.
   - B Tieneba mucho miedo.
   - C Tenía mucho miedo.
   - D Tenguía mucho miedo.

7. ¿Vienes a poner una denuncia?
   - A ¿Venías a poner una denuncia?
   - B ¿Venabas a poner una denuncia?
   - C ¿Vengabas a poner una denuncia?
   - D ¿Vienguías a poner una denuncia?

Unit 19
ESENCIALES

Answers page 185

| Tema | **The imperfect (irregular forms)** |

*Choose the correct imperfect form of **ser** or **estar** in each case.*

1. Los ladrones no ... del barrio.
   - A eran
   - B estaban

2. ... absolutamente convencidos de eso.
   - A Éramos
   - B Estábamos

3. ... un muchacho muy joven.
   - A Era
   - B Estaba

4. Mi cartera ... en un bolsillo.
   - A era
   - B estaba

5. ... usted muy equivocado.
   - A Era
   - B Estaba

6. ¿... altos los ladrones?
   - A Eran
   - B Estaban

7. ¿Dónde ...?
   - A eras
   - B estabas

8. Yo ... sentado en una silla.
   - A era
   - B estaba

9. ... españoles.
   - A Eran
   - B Estaban

10. ... tomando una copa.
    - A Éramos
    - B Estábamos

Select the correct imperfect form of the verb in each sentence.

Answers page 185

1. ¿Adónde vas?
   - A vaías
   - B ibas
   - C veías
   - D vías

2. No vemos el sol desde hace días.

   Ⓐ vaíamos   Ⓑ íbamos   Ⓒ veíamos   Ⓓ víamos

3. ¿Qué tal te va la vida?

   Ⓐ vaía   Ⓑ iba   Ⓒ veía   Ⓓ vía

4. ¿Vais a poner una denuncia?

   Ⓐ vaíais   Ⓑ ibais   Ⓒ veíais   Ⓓ víais

5. Sin gafas no veo nada.

   Ⓐ vaía   Ⓑ iba   Ⓒ veía   Ⓓ vía

6. Se ven durante los fines de semana.

   Ⓐ vaían   Ⓑ iban   Ⓒ veían   Ⓓ vían

Tema   **The preterite**

Choose the correct preterite forms of the verbs to transform these sentences into the past tense.

Answers
page 185

1. Relleno la declaración, escribo la fecha y firmo.

   Ⓐ Rellení / escribí / firmé   Ⓒ Rellené / escribé / firmí

   Ⓑ Rellené / escribí / firmé

2. Te disculpas y me ayudas.

   Ⓐ Te disculpaste / ayudaste   Ⓒ Te disculpiste / ayudiste

   Ⓑ Te disculpaste / ayudiste

3. Insiste en ayudarme y lleva él la bolsa.

   Ⓐ Insistió / llevó   Ⓒ Insistó / llevió

   Ⓑ Insistió / llevió

4. Encontramos una cartera en el suelo y la llevamos a comisaría.

   Ⓐ Encontramos / llevamos   Ⓒ Encontrimos / llevamos

   Ⓑ Encontramos / llevimos

Unit 19
ÚTILES

Verbs and expressions

callarse	*to keep quiet*
existir	*to exist*
firmar	*to sign*
insistir	*to insist*
llevarse	*to take or make off with something*
meter	*to put, to place into*
rellenar	*to fill, to stuff*
robar	*to steal something*
chocar con + object	*to run into, to crash into something*
cumplir x años	*to be x years old*
poner una denuncia	*to make a complaint, to file a police report*

Nouns

la bolsa	*bag* (plastic or paper shopping bag)
el bolsillo	*pocket* (in clothing)
el bolso	*handbag*
la cartera	*wallet*
el ladrón / la ladrona	*thief, robber* (m./f.)
el muchacho / la muchacha	*boy / girl*
la noticia	*news, announcement*
el sol	*sun*
el suelo	*ground, floor*

Adverbial phrases

al rato	*shortly afterwards*
de pronto	*suddenly*

ESENCIALES

PAGE 176
Pronunciation and spelling: ü
1 **A** 2 **B** 3 **A** 4 **B** 5 **A** 6 **A** 7 **B** 8 **A** 9 **A** 10 **B**

PAGE 177
Written accents
1 **B** 2 **A** 3 **A** 4 **B** 5 **A** 6 **B** 7 **B** 8 **A** 9 **A** 10 **B**

Containers and contents
1 **A** 2 **D** 3 **B** 4 **C**

PAGE 178
Commands
1 **A** 2 **C** 3 **A** 4 **C** 5 **C** 6 **A** 7 **C** 8 **A**

PAGE 179
The imperfect
1 **B** 2 **A** 3 **A** 4 **B** 5 **B** 6 **C** 7 **A**

PAGE 180
The imperfect (irregular forms)
1 **A** 2 **B** 3 **A** 4 **B** 5 **B** 6 **A** 7 **B** 8 **B** 9 **A** 10 **B**

1 **B** 2 **C** 3 **B** 4 **B** 5 **C** 6 **C**

PAGE 181
The preterite
1 **B** 2 **A** 3 **A** 4 **A** 5 **C** 6 **C** 7 **A**

PAGE 182
The preterite (irregular forms)
1 **B** 2 **B** 3 **A** 4 **C** 5 **C** 6 **B**

PAGE 183
Which past tense?
1 **C** 2 **C** 3 **B** 4 **D** 5 **A** 6 **D**

YOUR SCORE:

Did you get between 0 and 14? ¡Ay, ay, ay!

Did you get between 15 and 29? Muy justito...

Did you get between 30 and 44? No está mal, pero...

Did you get between 45 and 59? Enhorabuena.

Did you get 60 or over? ¡Eres un auténtico fenómeno!

Unit 20
ESENCIALES

Answers
page 195

Tema In-laws

Choose the correct term in each case.

1. El padre de mi mujer es mi...

   Ⓐ cuñado.   Ⓑ suegro.   Ⓒ yerno.

2. La mujer de mi hijo es mi...

   Ⓐ cuñada.   Ⓑ suegra.   Ⓒ nuera.

3. La hermana de mi mujer es mi...

   Ⓐ cuñada.   Ⓑ suegra.   Ⓒ nuera.

4. El marido de mi hija es mi...

   Ⓐ cuñado.   Ⓑ suegro.   Ⓒ yerno.

Tema Parts of the body

Select the ending of the word referring to parts of the body.

Answers
page 195

1. Me he roto el bra...

   Ⓐ ... sa.   Ⓑ ... zo.   Ⓒ ... co.

2. Dame la ma...

   Ⓐ ... na.   Ⓑ ... ni.   Ⓒ ... no.

3. Tiene pier... largas.

   Ⓐ ... nas   Ⓑ ... las   Ⓒ ... tas

4. Te pido perdón de rodi...

   Ⓐ ... los.   Ⓑ ... llas.   Ⓒ ... llos.

5. Tengo de... de pianista.

   Ⓐ ... dos   Ⓑ ... das   Ⓒ ... tos

Now select the beginning of the word referring to parts of the body.

1. Llevo el reloj en la ...ca izquierda.

   Ⓐ meñi ...   Ⓑ muñe...   Ⓒ miña...

Answers
page 195

2. Un pie tiene veintiséis ...sos.

   Ⓐ ho...   Ⓑ o...   Ⓒ hue...

3. Me he torcido el ...llo.

   Ⓐ chevi...   Ⓑ tobi...   Ⓒ chovi...

4. Cúbrete el ...llo.

   Ⓐ cue...   Ⓑ co...   Ⓒ cui...

Tema | **It hurts ...**

Based on the elements provided, select the correctly constructed sentence.

1. nosotros / doler / la garganta

   Answers page 195

   Ⓐ Nos dolemos la garganta.

   Ⓑ Nos duele la garganta.

   Ⓒ A nosotros nos duelen la garganta.

2. ellos / doler / la cabeza

   Ⓐ A ellos se les duele la garganta.

   Ⓑ Duelen la cabeza.

   Ⓒ Les duele la cabeza.

3. yo / doler / los dientes

   Ⓐ A mí me duelen los dientes.

   Ⓑ Duelo los dientes.

   Ⓒ Me duele los dientes.

4. tú / doler / los oídos

   Ⓐ Te duelen los oídos.

   Ⓑ Te dueles los oídos.

   Ⓒ Ti duelen los oídos.

5. usted / doler / la nariz

   (A) A usted se le duele la nariz.

   (B) Le duele la nariz.

   (C) A usted se duele la nariz.

6. vosotros / doler / los ojos

   (A) A vosotros doléis los ojos.

   (B) Os duelen los ojos.

   (C) Vos doléis los ojos.

Tema **The preterite (irregular forms)**

*Select the correct preterite (simple past) form of the verb **querer** to complete these sentences.*

Answer page 1?

1. ¿Por qué no ... ir al médico?

   (A) quisistes   (B) quisite   (C) quisiste   (D) quisiteis

2. Mi suegra no ... ayudarme.

   (A) quise   (B) quiso   (C) quisé   (D) quisó

3. Yo no ... llevarla al médico.

   (A) quise   (B) quiso   (C) quisé   (D) quisó

4. No ... movernos en todo el fin de semana.

   (A) quisiemos   (B) quisismos   (C) quiesimos   (D) quisimos

5. No ... bañarse.

   (A) quesieron   (B) quieseron   (C) quisieron   (D) quiseron

6. ¿Por qué no ... venir con nosotros?

   (A) quisistis   (B) quisiestis   (C) quisiteis   (D) quisisteis

Choose the equivalent in the preterite tense for each of these sentences.

1. ¿Vas a la playa hoy?

   A ¿Viste a la playa ayer?

   B ¿Fuiste a la playa ayer?

   C ¿Fuites a la playa ayer?

Answers page 195

2. No sois prudentes.

   A No fuisteis prudentes.

   B No fuistes prudentes.

   C No fuiteis prudentes.

3. Estas vacaciones son horribles.

   A Aquellas vacaciones fueron horribles.

   B Aquellas vacaciones fieron horribles.

   C Aquellas vacaciones fuyeron horribles.

4. Voy a casa de mi cuñado a hacer una barbacoa.

   A Fuo a casa de mi cuñado a hacer una barbacoa.

   B Fue a casa de mi cuñado a hacer una barbacoa.

   C Fui a casa de mi cuñado a hacer una barbacoa.

5. Mi cumpleaños es hoy.

   A Mi cumpleaños fuo anteayer.

   B Mi cumpleaños fue anteayer.

   C Mi cumpleaños fui anteayer.

6. Vamos a tomar el sol esta tarde.

   A Fuimos a tomar el sol ayer tarde.

   B Vimos a tomar el sol ayer tarde.

   C Fuemos a tomar el sol ayer tarde.

Choose the equivalent in the preterite tense for each of these sentences in the present perfect.

Answers
page 195

1. Pedro no ha tenido vacaciones este año.

   Ⓐ El año pasado Pedro no tuvo vacaciones.

   Ⓑ El año pasado Pedro no tuve vacaciones.

2. He tenido que ir al médico hoy.

   Ⓐ La semana pasada tuvo que ir al médico.

   Ⓑ La semana pasada tuve que ir al médico.

3. ¿Has tenido un accidente esta mañana?

   Ⓐ ¿Tuviste un accidente ayer?

   Ⓑ ¿Tuvistes un accidente ayer?

4. No han tenido cuidado y se han puesto enfermos.

   Ⓐ No tuveron cuidado y se ponieron enfermos.

   Ⓑ No tuvieron cuidado y se pusieron enfermos.

5. ¿Por qué no os habéis puesto un sombrero?

   Ⓐ ¿Por qué no os pusisteis un sombrero?

   Ⓑ ¿Por qué no os pusiteis un sombrero?

Tema	**Perfect tenses**

Choose the correct perfect tense for each context.

Answers
page 195

1. Creía que te ... el brazo.

   Ⓐ hayas roto   Ⓑ habías roto

2. No pienso que ... una buena idea.

   Ⓐ haya sido   Ⓑ había sido

3. ¿No ... que os quedabais en casa?

   Ⓐ hayáis dicho   Ⓑ habías dicho

4. Lo siento, no me ... de tu enfermedad.

   Ⓐ haya enterado   Ⓑ había enterado

5. Quiero que ... de comer a las tres, ¿vale?

   Ⓐ hayamos terminado   Ⓑ habíamos terminado

6. No contestan, quizás ...

   Ⓐ hayan salido.   Ⓑ habían salido.

Tema   **At the doctor's**

Select the corresponding sentence in Spanish in each case. More than one option may be possible.

Answers page 195

1. I have a cold.

   Ⓐ Estoy resfriado.   Ⓑ Estoy acatarrado.   Ⓒ Estoy constipado.

2. I have a cough.

   Ⓐ Tengo de la tox.   Ⓑ Tengo tos.   Ⓒ Tengo tox.

3. Do you have a prescription?

   Ⓐ ¿Tiene usted una receta?

   Ⓑ ¿Tiene usted una ordenanza?

   Ⓒ ¿Tiene usted una orden?

4. I'm going to prescribe an antibiotic for you.

   Ⓐ Le voy a describir un antibiótico.

   Ⓑ Le voy a ordenar un antibiótico.

   Ⓒ Le voy a recetar un antibiótico.

5. I cut myself.

   Ⓐ Me he mareado.   Ⓑ Me he caído.   Ⓒ Me he cortado.

6. I would like some cotton pads and a bandage.

   Ⓐ Quisiera cotón y un venda.

   Ⓑ Quisiera algodón y una venda.

   Ⓒ Quisiera alcotón y un vendo.

| Tema | Contrast or consequence |

Select the most suitable connecting phrase to link the two parts of each sentence, conveying either contrast (however, whereas) or consequence (so, therefore).

1. Lo de usted no es grave, ... su suegra sí necesita ir al hospital.
   - **A** en cambio
   - **B** por lo tanto

2. Mi suegra se pone morena enseguida. Yo, ..., no lo consigo.
   - **A** en cambio
   - **B** por lo tanto

3. Se ha roto el brazo. Voy a tener ... que ponerle una escayola.
   - **A** en cambio
   - **B** por lo tanto

4. Tiene usted un fuerte catarro. ... le aconsejo que guarde cama unos días.
   - **A** En cambio
   - **B** Por lo tanto

5. El corte en el dedo es superficial. ... basta con una tirita.
   - **A** En cambio
   - **B** Por lo tanto

6. El corte en el dedo es superficial. ... le voy a recetar una crema para las quemaduras de la espalda.
   - **A** En cambio
   - **B** Por lo tanto

| Verbs and expressions | ÚTILES |

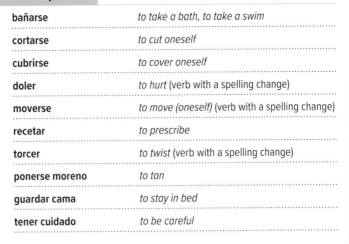

bañarse	*to take a bath, to take a swim*
cortarse	*to cut oneself*
cubrirse	*to cover oneself*
doler	*to hurt* (verb with a spelling change)
moverse	*to move (oneself)* (verb with a spelling change)
recetar	*to prescribe*
torcer	*to twist* (verb with a spelling change)
ponerse moreno	*to tan*
guardar cama	*to stay in bed*
tener cuidado	*to be careful*

In-laws

la familia política	*in-laws*
el cuñado / la cuñada	*brother-in-law / sister-in-law*
la nuera	*daughter-in-law*
el suegro / la suegra	*father-in-law / mother-in-law*
el yerno	*son-in-law*

Parts of the body

el brazo	*arm*
el cuello	*neck*
el dedo	*finger*
la garganta	*throat*
el hueso	*bone*
la mano	*hand*
la muñeca	*wrist*
la pierna	*leg*
la rodilla	*knee*
el tobillo	*ankle*

At the doctor's

estar acatarrado/a	*to have a cold* (m./f.)
estar constipado/a	*to have a cold* (m./f.)
estar resfriado/a	*to have a cold* (m./f.)
el catarro	*cold* (illness)
un corte	*a cut*

Unit 20
ÚTILES

el algodón	*cotton*
la crema	*cream, ointment*
la enfermedad	*illness, sickness*
una escayola	*plaster cast*
el hospital	*hospital*
la quemadura	*burn*
la receta	*prescription*
una tirita	*sticking plaster, band-aid*
la tos	*cough*
una venda	*bandage*

Holidays

la barbacoa	*barbecue*
el mar	*sea, ocean*
la playa	*beach*
el sombrero	*hat*
las vacaciones	*vacation, holiday*

Adverbs of time

anteayer	*day before yesterday*
ayer	*yesterday*
ayer tarde	*yesterday evening*
enseguida	*right away, immediately*

Connecting words

en cambio	*however, whereas*
por lo tanto	*so, therefore*

ESENCIALES

PAGE 186
In-laws
1 **B** 2 **C** 3 **A** 4 **C**

PAGE 186
Parts of the body
1 **B** 2 **C** 3 **A** 4 **B** 5 **A**
1 **B** 2 **C** 3 **B** 4 **A**

PAGE 187
It hurts ...
1 **B** 2 **C** 3 **A** 4 **A** 5 **B** 6 **B**

PAGE 188
The preterite (irregular forms)
1 **C** 2 **B** 3 **A** 4 **D** 5 **C** 6 **D**
1 **B** 2 **A** 3 **A** 4 **C** 5 **B** 6 **A**
1 **A** 2 **B** 3 **A** 4 **B** 5 **A**

PAGE 190
Perfect tenses
1 **B** 2 **A** 3 **B** 4 **B** 5 **A** 6 **A**

PAGE 191
At the doctor's
1 **A**, **B** et **C** 2 **B** 3 **A** 4 **C** 5 **C** 6 **B**

PAGE 192
Contrast or consequence
1 **A** 2 **A** 3 **B** 4 **B** 5 **B** 6 **A**

YOUR
SCORE:

Did you get between 0 and 10? ¡Ay, ay, ay!

Did you get between 11 and 21? Muy justito...

Did you get between 22 and 32? No está mal, pero...

Did you get between 33 and 43? Enhorabuena.

Did you get 44 or over? ¡Eres un auténtico fenómeno!

Unit 21
ESENCIALES

Tema Spelling

Choose the correct plural equivalent in each case.

Answers page 206

1. Mi animal preferido es el pez.

   A Mis animales preferidos son los peses.

   B Mis animales preferidos son los pezes.

   C Mis animales preferidos son los peces.

2. No soy capaz de hacerlo.

   A No somos capazes de hacerlo.

   B No somos capaces de hacerlo.

   C No somos capases de hacerlo.

3. Tengo un amigo barcelonés.

   A Tengo amigos barceloneses.

   B Tengo amigos barceloneces.

   C Tengo amigos barcelonezes.

4. He ido a España una sola vez.

   A He ido a España varias vezes.

   B He ido a España varias veses.

   C He ido a España varias veces.

5. Me encanta el autobús.

   A Me encantan los autobuzes.

   B Me encantan los autobuces.

   C Me encantan los autobuses.

Choose the correct spelling of these superlative adjectives.

Answers page 206

1. ¡Felices fiestas!

   A ¡Felicísimas fiestas!

   B ¡Felizísimas fiestas!

   C ¡Felisísimas fiestas!

   D ¡Feliquísimas fiestas!

2. Las gambas están frescas.

   A Las gambas están frescísimas.   C Las gambas están fresquísimas.

   B Las gambas están fressísimas   D Las gambas están freskísimas.

3. Hay poca gente.

   A Hay poquísima gente.   C Hay pokísima gente.

   B Hay pocísima gente.   D Hay posísima gente.

4. La cola es larga.

   A La cola es largüísima.   C La cola es largísima.

   B La cola es larguízima.   D La cola es larguísima.

5. Este pescado está rico.

   A Este pescado está riquísimo.   C Este pescado está rikísimo.

   B Este pescado está rizísimo   D Este pescado está ricísimo.

Select the option with the correct diminutive of the noun.

Answers page 206

1. ¡Qué nariz más bonita!

   A ¡Qué narizita más bonita!

   B ¡Qué narisita más bonita!

   C ¡Qué naricita más bonita!

   D ¡Qué narissita más bonita!

2. Me encantan las plazas de Cádiz.

   A Me encantan las placitas de Cádiz.

   B Me encantan las plazitas de Cádiz

   C Me encantan las plassitas de Cádiz.

   D Me encantan las plasitas de Cádiz.

3. Es una muchacha encantadora.

    Ⓐ Es una muchacita encantadora.

    Ⓑ Es una muchakita encantadora.

    Ⓒ Es una muchaquita encantadora.

    Ⓓ Es una muchachita encantadora.

4. ¿A cuánto está el marisco hoy?

    Ⓐ ¿A cuánto está el mariskito hoy?

    Ⓑ ¿A cuánto está el marisquito hoy?

    Ⓒ ¿A cuánto está el mariscito hoy?

    Ⓓ ¿A cuánto está el maricito hoy?

5. Mi hija tiene muchas amigas.

    Ⓐ Mi hija tiene muchas amijitas.

    Ⓑ Mi hija tiene muchas amigüitas.

    Ⓒ Mi hija tiene muchas amiguitas.

    Ⓓ Mi hija tiene muchas amigitas.

Tema **Asking the price**

Select the appropriate option to complete the question. More than one answer may be possible.

Answers page 206

1. ¿... cuesta una paella en este restaurante?

    Ⓐ A cuánto   Ⓑ Cómo   Ⓒ Cuánto

    Ⓓ A qué   Ⓔ Qué

2. ¿A ... están los calamares?

    Ⓐ a cuánto   Ⓑ cómo   Ⓒ cuánto

    Ⓓ a qué   Ⓔ qué

3. ¿... precio están las gambas?

    Ⓐ A cuánto   Ⓑ Cómo   Ⓒ Cuánto

    Ⓓ A qué   Ⓔ Qué

4. ¿... está el kilo de mejillones?

   A A cuánto   B Cómo   C Cuánto

   D A qué   E Qué

5. ¿... precio está el pollo de granja?

   A A cuánto   B Cómo   C Cuánto

   D A qué   E Qué

6. ¿... precio tienen las naranjas?

   A A cuánto   B Cómo   C Cuánto

   D A qué   E Qué

Tema   **Thanking**

Choose the equivalent in Spanish. More than one option may be possible.

Answers page 206

1. Thank him.

   A Agradécele.

   B Dale las gracias.

2. You don't have to thank me.

   A No me tienes que agradecer.

   B No me tienes que dar las gracias.

3. The neighbours thank us.

   A Los vecinos nos agradecen.

   B Los vecinos nos dan las gracias.

4. Thank you for your gift.

   A Te agradezco por tu regalo.

   B Te agradezco tu regalo.

   C Te doy las gracias por tu regalo.

Unit 21
ESENCIALES

5. The neighbours thank us for what we did.

A Los vecinos nos agradecen lo que hemos hecho.

B Los vecinos nos agradecen por lo que hemos hecho.

C Los vecinos nos dan las gracias por lo que hemos hecho.

Tema **Waiting in line**

Choose the correct option to complete the sentence. More than one may be right.

1. Si soy el último en una cola y entra un cliente, ...

A le pido la vez. B le doy la vez.

Answers page 206

2. Si llego a una tienda y hay clientes, ...

A pido la vez. B doy la vez.

3. Si llego a una tienda y hay clientes, ...

A hago cola. B hago la cola. C hago la ola.

4. Si llego a una tienda y hay clientes, pregunto:

A ¿Quién es el último? B ¿Quién va? C ¿A quién le toca?

5. Si llega mi turno, digo:

A Voy yo. B Me toca a mí. C ¿Quién da la vez?

Tema **Prepositions of time and place**

Select the most appropriate preposition for each context.

Answers page 206

1. Me lavo los dientes ... comer.

A antes de B delante de C después de D detrás de

2. Me lavo las manos ... comer.

A antes de B delante de C después de D detrás de

3. Suelo cenar ... la tele.

A antes de B delante de C después de D detrás de

4. ... comer, siempre tengo ganas de echar la siesta.

   A Antes de   **B** Delante de   **C** Después de   **D** Detrás de

5. Hagan cola, por favor, uno ... otro.

   A antes de   **B** delante de   **C** después de   **D** detrás de

---

Tema **The preterite (irregular forms)**

Select the correct equivalent in the preterite.

Answers page 206

1. Hoy he estado en casa toda la mañana.

   A Ayer estuvo en casa toda la mañana.

   B Ayer estuve en casa toda la mañana.

   C Ayer estuvi en casa toda la mañana.

   D Ayer estuvó en casa toda la mañana.

2. Este año Pedro está en el paro.

   A El año pasado Pedro estuvo en el paro.

   B El año pasado Pedro estuve en el paro.

   C El año pasado Pedro estuvó en el paro.

   D El año pasado Pedro estuvé en el paro.

3. ¿Dónde habéis estado esta mañana?

   A ¿Dónde estuviteis anoche?

   B ¿Dónde estuvistes anoche?

   C ¿Dónde estuvisteis anoche?

   D ¿Dónde estuvistis anoche?

4. ¿Eres tú el que llama todas las noches?

   A ¿Estuvistes tú el que llamó anteanoche?

   B ¿Fuistes tú el que llamó anteanoche?

   C ¿Estuviste tú el que llamó anteanoche?

   D ¿Fuiste tú el que llamó anteanoche?

Unit 21
ÚTILES

Thanking

agradecer	*to thank for* (This verb is transitive and requires an object referring to what the person is grateful about: **agradezco** on its own is meaningless. It is constructed with two objects to indicate who is being thanked and for what: **Te agradezco tu ayuda.** / *thank you for your help.*)
dar las gracias	*to thank* (This expression can be used without an object: **Doy las gracias.** *Thanks.* When it is used with an object referring to what the person is grateful about, this is introduced with **por**: **Te doy las gracias por tu ayuda.** / *I thank you for your help.*)

Waiting in line

hacer cola	*to line up, to queue*
pedir la vez	*to ask who is the last person in the queue*
dar la vez	*to say one is the last in the queue*
¿A quién le toca? or **¿Quién va?**	*Whose turn is it?* (a shopkeeper to the customers who are waiting)
Me toca a mí. / Te toca a ti. / Le toca a él.	*It's my / your / his turn.*
Voy yo. / Va usted.	*I'm next. / You go ahead.*

Asking the price

¿Cuánto cuesta(n)...?	*How much does/do the ... cost?*
¿Qué precio tiene(n)...?	*What's the price of the ...?* (sing./pl.)
¿A cuánto está(n)...? / ¿A cómo está(n)...?	*How much is/are the ...?*

Seafood

a la plancha	*grilled, griddled*
a la sal	*in salt*
el calamar	*squid*

el mejillón	*mussel*
frito/a	*fried* (m./f.)
la gamba	*prawn*
la lubina	*sea bass*
el marisco	*shellfish, seafood*
el arroz con marisco	*rice with seafood*
la pescadería	*fish market*
el pescado	*fish* (food)
el pez	*fish* (animal)

Adverbs and prepositions of time

anoche	*last night*
anteanoche	*night before last*
anteayer	*day before yesterday*
antes	*before* (adv.)
antes de	*before* (prep.)
ayer	*yesterday*
después	*after* (adv.)
después de	*after* (prep.)
el año pasado	*last year*
hoy	*today*
luego	*later, afterwards*

Adverbs and prepositions of place

delante	*in front* (adv.)
delante de	*in front of* (prep.)
detrás	*behind* (adv.)
detrás de	*behind* (prep.)

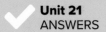

Unit 21
ANSWERS

ESENCIALES

PAGE 196
Spelling
1 **C** 2 **B** 3 **A** 4 **C** 5 **C**
1 **A** 2 **C** 3 **A** 4 **D** 5 **A**
1 **C** 2 **A** 3 **D** 4 **B** 5 **C**

PAGE 198
Asking the price
1 **C**, **E** 2 **B**, **C** 3 **D** 4 **A** 5 **D** 6 **E**

PAGE 199
Thanking
1 **B** 2 **B** 3 **B** 4 **B**, **C** 5 **A**, **C**

PAGE 200
Waiting in line
1 **B** 2 **A** 3 **A** 4 **A** 5 **A**, **B**

Prepositions of time and place
1 **C** 2 **A** 3 **B** 4 **C** 5 **D**

PAGE 201
The preterite (irregular forms)
1 **B** 2 **A** 3 **C** 4 **D** 5 **A**
1 **D** 2 **A** 3 **A** 4 **D** 5 **D** 6 **C**
1 **A** 2 **C** 3 **B** 4 **B** 5 **C** 6 **B**

YOUR SCORE:

Did you get between 0 and 10? ¡Ay, ay, ay!

Did you get between 11 and 21? Muy justito...

Did you get between 22 and 32? No está mal, pero...

Did you get between 33 and 43? Enhorabuena.

Did you get 44 or over? ¡Eres un auténtico fenómeno!

Tema Shopping

Answers
page 218

Choose the correct ending for the name of the shop.

1. Compro pan en la pana...

   Ⓐ ...cería.   Ⓑ ...dería.   Ⓒ ...ería.   Ⓓ ...lería.

2. Compro carne en la carni...

   Ⓐ ...cería.   Ⓑ ...dería.   Ⓒ ...ería.   Ⓓ ...tería.

3. Compro salchichón en la charcu...

   Ⓐ ...cería.   Ⓑ ...dería.   Ⓒ ...lería.   Ⓓ ...tería.

4. Compro verdura en la verdu...

   Ⓐ ...dería.   Ⓑ ...lería.   Ⓒ ...rería.   Ⓓ ...tería.

5. Compro pescado en la pesca...

   Ⓐ ...dería.   Ⓑ ...ería.   Ⓒ ...lería.   Ⓓ ...tería.

6. Compro fruta en la fru...

   Ⓐ ...cería.   Ⓑ ...dería.   Ⓒ ...ería.   Ⓓ ...tería.

Tema Types of food

*Select the category (**legumbre** pulse or **verdura** vegetable) of each food.*

1. el garbanzo

   Ⓐ legumbre   Ⓑ verdura

Answers
page 218

2. la cebolla

   Ⓐ legumbre   Ⓑ verdura

3. el puerro

   Ⓐ legumbre   Ⓑ verdura

4. la alubia

   Ⓐ legumbre   Ⓑ verdura

5. la lenteja

   Ⓐ legumbre   Ⓑ verdura

6. la zanahoria

   A legumbre   B verdura

7. el pimiento

   A legumbre   B verdura

*Select the category (**fruta** fruit or **fruto seco** dried fruit or nuts) of each food.*

1. la avellana

   A fruta   B fruto seco

Answers page 218

2. la nuez

   A fruta   B fruto seco

3. el melocotón

   A fruta   B fruto seco

4. el cacahuete

   A fruta   B fruto seco

5. el plátano

   A fruta   B fruto seco

6. la pasa

   A fruta   B fruto seco

7. la pera

   A fruta   B fruto seco

8. la manzana

   A fruta   B fruto seco

9. la piña

   A fruta   B fruto seco

10. la uva

    A fruta   B fruto seco

11. la almendra

    A fruta   B fruto seco

12. la cereza

- Ⓐ fruta
- Ⓑ fruto seco

Tema Products and packaging

Select the packaging that corresponds to each product. More than one option may be possible.

Answers
page 218

1. ... de papel higiénico
   - Ⓐ Un rollo
   - Ⓑ Un tarro
   - Ⓒ Un tubo
   - Ⓓ Una lata

2. ... de patatas fritas
   - Ⓐ Un tubo
   - Ⓑ Una bolsa
   - Ⓒ Una botella
   - Ⓓ Una lata

3. ... de pasta de dientes
   - Ⓐ Un rollo
   - Ⓑ Un tarro
   - Ⓒ Un tubo
   - Ⓓ Una lata

4. ... de vino
   - Ⓐ Un cartón
   - Ⓑ Un tubo
   - Ⓒ Una bolsa
   - Ⓓ Una botella

5. ... de cerveza
   - Ⓐ Un rollo
   - Ⓑ Un tarro
   - Ⓒ Una botella
   - Ⓓ Una lata

6. ... de mermelada
   - Ⓐ Un paquete
   - Ⓑ Un tarro
   - Ⓒ Una bolsa
   - Ⓓ Una lata

7. ... de detergente
   - Ⓐ Un paquete
   - Ⓑ Un rollo
   - Ⓒ Una bolsa
   - Ⓓ Una botella

8. ... de champú
   - Ⓐ Un rollo
   - Ⓑ Un tubo
   - Ⓒ Una bolsa
   - Ⓓ Una lata

9. ... de leche
   - Ⓐ Un cartón
   - Ⓑ Un rollo
   - Ⓒ Una bolsa
   - Ⓓ Una botella

10. ... de sardinas
    - Ⓐ Un rollo
    - Ⓑ Un tubo
    - Ⓒ Una bolsa
    - Ⓓ Una lata

Unit 22
ESENCIALES

Tema Objects and materials

Select the material each object is made from. More than one option may be possible.

Answers page 218

1. Un vaso...

   Ⓐ de plástico   Ⓑ de cristal   Ⓒ de lana

2. Un jersey...

   Ⓐ de papel   Ⓑ de lana   Ⓒ de madera

3. Una camisa...

   Ⓐ de hierro   Ⓑ de piedra   Ⓒ de algodón

4. Una silla...

   Ⓐ de madera   Ⓑ de papel   Ⓒ de algodón

5. Una puerta...

   Ⓐ de papel   Ⓑ de hierro   Ⓒ de algodón

6. Una mesa...

   Ⓐ de piedra   Ⓑ de madera   Ⓒ de papel

7. Una cazadora...

   Ⓐ de lana   Ⓑ de cristal   Ⓒ de cuero

8. Una bolsa...

   Ⓐ de plástico   Ⓑ de papel   Ⓒ de hierro

Tema *Ser* or *estar*?

Choose the correct verb for each context.

Answers page 218

1. Las gambas ... más ricas con un poquito de sal y limón.

   Ⓐ son   Ⓑ están

2. No todas las españolas ... morenas y de ojos negros.

   Ⓐ son   Ⓑ están

3. No ... bastante rico para ir a este restaurante.

   Ⓐ soy   Ⓑ estoy

4. Cuando no ... fresco, el pescado huele mal.

   Ⓐ es　　　　　　　　　Ⓑ está

5. Estas sardinas, ¿... frescas o congeladas?

   Ⓐ son　　　　　　　　Ⓑ están

6. No hay que comer manzanas si ... verdes.

   Ⓐ están　　　　　　　Ⓑ son

7. Tus ojos ... verdes como la hierba.

   Ⓐ son　　　　　　　　Ⓑ están

8. Ya ... listo, ¿vamos?

   Ⓐ soy　　　　　　　　Ⓑ estoy

9. ... más listo que su hermano.

   Ⓐ Es　　　　　　　　Ⓑ Está

10. ¡... muy morena! ¿Has ido a la playa?

    Ⓐ Eres　　　　　　　Ⓑ Estás

Choose the correct verb for each context.

1. Comer demasiada mantequilla no ... bueno para el corazón.

   Ⓐ es　　　　　　　　Ⓑ está

Answers page 218

2. ¡Puaj! ¡Estos cruasanes no ... buenos!

   Ⓐ son　　　　　　　　Ⓑ están

3. Estos precocinados ... malísimos: no sé cómo puedes comértelos.

   Ⓐ son　　　　　　　　Ⓑ están

4. ... malísimos para la salud.

   Ⓐ Son　　　　　　　Ⓑ Están

5. Mira la fecha de estos yogures y dime si todavía ... buenos.

   Ⓐ son　　　　　　　　Ⓑ están

6. Me encantan los yogures y además ... buenos para la digestión.

   Ⓐ son　　　　　　　　Ⓑ están

7. ... malo, tengo un fuerte catarro.

   A Soy

   B Estoy

8. ¡Qué malo ... cocinando!

   A eres

   B estás

9. ... bueno echarse una siesta después de comer.

   A Es

   B Está

10. No me cae bien. ... malo y antipático.

   A Es

   B Está

Tema *Llevar* (take) or *traer* (bring)?

Choose the most suitable verb to complete each sentence.

Answers page 218

1. ¡... a Sevilla, por favor!

   A Llévame

   B Tráeme

2. Si vas al súper, ... cervezas.

   A lleva

   B trae

3. Mira, te hemos ... un regalo.

   A llevado

   B traído

4. Escúchame, ... buenas noticias.

   A llevo

   B traigo

5. Tengo coche, ¿quieres que te ... a alguna parte?

   A lleve

   B traiga

6. Si vas a hacer la compra, ... una lista.

   A llévate

   B tráete

7. Hacemos una barbacoa en casa, ... vosotros las bebidas, ¿vale?

   A llevad

   B traed

8. Está en la cama y no puede moverse, ... el periódico.

   A llévale

   B tráele

Tema   The preterite (irregular forms)

Choose the correct preterite verb form(s) to complete each sentence.

1. Mis abuelos siempre ... la compra en las tiendas de barrio.
   - A hiceron
   - B hizieron
   - C hacieron
   - D hicieron

2. Ayer ... pasta con gambas.
   - A hacimos
   - B hazimos
   - C hicimos
   - D hizimos

3. Finalmente, ¿cómo ... el marisco?
   - A hicisteis
   - B hacisteis
   - C hizisteis
   - D hicistes

4. Lo ... yo solo, no me ... falta ayuda de nadie.
   - A hico / hize
   - B hací / hació
   - C hizo / hice
   - D hice / hizo

5. Se te ha olvidado casi todo, ¿por qué no ... una lista?
   - A hacistes
   - B hiciste
   - C hiziste
   - D hicistes

Select the correct verb to convey that the action happened in the past.

Answers
page 218

1. ¿Por qué traes esos precocinados asquerosos?
   - A traístes
   - B traíste
   - C trajiste
   - D trajistes

2. Te traigo el zumo de naranja que te gusta.
   - A trajo
   - B traje
   - C traí
   - D trají

3. Traen un montón de cosas inútiles del súper.
   - A trajiron
   - B trajieron
   - C trajeron
   - D trayeron

4. ¿Qué te digo siempre?
   - A dijó
   - B dijé
   - C dijo
   - D dije

5. ¿Y los vecinos no te dicen nada?
   - A dijieron
   - B dijeron
   - C dejeron
   - D dejieron

6. Mi abuela italiana nunca me dice cómo hacer la pasta.
   - A dijó
   - B dijé
   - C dijo
   - D dije

Verbs

cocinar	*to cook*
llevar	*to take, to carry* (indicates movement <u>away from</u> the location of the person who is speaking; the related verb is **ir** *to go*)
traer	*to bring* (indicates movement <u>towards</u> the location of the person who is speaking; the related verb is **venir** *to come*)

Meanings of *ser* and *estar* + adjective

ser bueno/a	*to be good or nice* (personality traits), *to be good for one's health*
estar bueno/a	*to be in good health, to taste good*
ser malo/a	*to be mean, to be bad* (in quality, for one's health)
estar malo/a	*to be ill, to taste bad*
ser moreno/a	*to be dark-haired*
estar moreno/a	*to be tan*
ser rico/a	*to be rich*
estar rico/a	*to taste good*
ser verde, azul, ...	*to be green, blue...* (a lasting characteristic, e.g. to describe grass or the sky in a universal way)
estar verde, azul, ...	*to be green, blue...* (a changing characteristic, e.g. an unripe apple, or the sky at a particular time)
ser listo/a	*to be intelligent*
estar listo/a	*to be ready*

Vegetables and pulses

la verdura	*vegetables*
las legumbres	*pulses, legumes*
el garbanzo	*chickpea*
la alubia	*kidney bean*

la cebolla	*onion*
la judía verde	*green bean*
la lenteja	*lentil*
el pimiento	*pepper*
el puerro	*leek*
la zanahoria	*carrot*

Fruits and nuts

la fruta	*fruit*
los frutos secos	*dried fruit, nuts*
la almendra	*almond*
la avellana	*hazelnut*
el cacahuete	*peanut*
la cereza	*cherry*
el limón	*lemon*
la manzana	*apple*
el melocotón	*peach*
la nuez	*walnut, nut* (generic term)
la pasa	*raisin*
la pera	*pear*
la piña	*pineapple*
el plátano	*banana*
la uva	*grape*

Shops and professions

la carnicería / carnicero/a	*butcher shop / butcher* (m./f.)
la panadería / panadero/a	*bakery / baker* (m./f.)

Unit 22
ÚTILES

la pescadería / pescadero/a	*fish market / fisherman* (m./f.)
la verdulería / verdulero/a	*produce market / vegetable seller* (m./f.)
la frutería / frutero/a	*fruit stand / fruit seller* (m./f.)

Packaging

la botella	*bottle*
el cartón	*carton, box*
la lata	*tin, can*
el paquete	*package*
el rollo	*roll*
el tarro	*jar*
el tubo	*tube*
una bolsa	*sack, bag* (paper or plastic)

Provisions and toiletries

la bebida	*drink, beverage*
la cerveza	*beer*
el champú	*shampoo*
el cruasán	*croissant*
el detergente	*detergent*
la mermelada	*jam, jelly*
el papel higiénico	*toilet paper*
el salchichón	*salami* (cured sausage)
el vino	*wine*
el yogur	*yoghurt*
el zumo	*juice*

Materials

el algodón	*cotton*
el cristal	*glass, crystal*
el cuero	*leather*
el hierro	*iron*
la lana	*wool*
la madera	*wood*
el papel	*paper*
la piedra	*rock, stone*
el plástico	*plastic*

Nouns and adjectives

asqueroso/a	*disgusting* (m./f.)
el corazón	*heart*
la digestión	*digestion*
el jersey	*jumper, pullover, sweater*
el montón	*pile*
la puerta	*door*
la salud	*health*
el súper	*supermarket* (abbreviation of **supermercado**)

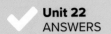

Unit 22
ANSWERS

ESENCIALES

PAGE 207
Shopping
1 **B** 2 **A** 3 **D** 4 **B** 5 **A** 6 **D**

Types of food
1 **A** 2 **B** 3 **B** 4 **A** 5 **A** 6 **B** 7 **B**
1 **B** 2 **B** 3 **A** 4 **B** 5 **A** 6 **B** 7 **A** 8 **A** 9 **A** 10 **A** 11 **B** 12 **A**

PAGE 209
Products and packaging
1 **A** 2 **B** 3 **C** 4 **A, D** 5 **C, D** 6 **B** 7 **A, D** 8 **B** 9 **A, D** 10 **D**

PAGE 210
Objects and materials
1 **A, B** 2 **B** 3 **C** 4 **A** 5 **B** 6 **A, B** 7 **A, C** 8 **A, B**

Ser or *estar*?
1 **B** 2 **A** 3 **A** 4 **B** 5 **A** 6 **A** 7 **A** 8 **B** 9 **A** 10 **B**
1 **A** 2 **B** 3 **B** 4 **A** 5 **B** 6 **A** 7 **B** 8 **A** 9 **A** 10 **A**

PAGE 212
Llevar (take) or *traer* (bring)?
1 **A** 2 **B** 3 **B** 4 **B** 5 **A** 6 **A** 7 **B** 8 **A**

PAGE 213
The preterite (irregular forms)
1 **D** 2 **C** 3 **A** 4 **D** 5 **B**
1 **C** 2 **B** 3 **C** 4 **D** 5 **B** 6 **C**

YOUR
SCORE:

Did you get between 0 and 15? ¡Ay, ay, ay!

Did you get between 16 and 31? Muy justito...

Did you get between 32 and 47? No está mal, pero...

Did you get between 48 and 63? Enhorabuena.

Did you get 64 or over? ¡Eres un auténtico fenómeno!

Tema **What day is it?**

Choose the correct option in each case. More than one may be possible.

1. ¿... día es hoy?

   (A) A qué

   (B) Qué

Answers page 228

2. ¿... día estamos?

   (A) A qué

   (B) Qué

3. ¿Qué día ... hoy?

   (A) estamos

   (B) somos

   (C) es

   (D) está

4. ¿A qué día ... hoy?

   (A) estamos

   (B) somos

   (C) es

   (D) está

5. Hoy ... lunes.

   (A) estamos a

   (B) somos a

   (C) estamos

   (D) somos

6. Hoy ... jueves.

   (A) es

   (B) es a

   (C) está

   (D) está a

7. Ayer ... martes.

   (A) estábamos

   (B) estábamos a

   (C) éramos

   (D) éramos a

8. Ayer ... sábado.

   (A) era a

   (B) estaba a

   (C) era

   (D) estábamos a

Unit 23
ESENCIALES

Select the date for each of these holidays in Spain.

1. Día de la Constitución
   - (A) uno de febrero
   - (B) ocho de diciembre
   - (C) veintiuno de junio

   Answers page 228

2. Día de los Inocentes
   - (A) uno de abril
   - (B) veintiocho de diciembre
   - (C) uno de agosto

3. Día de Reyes
   - (A) seis de enero
   - (B) treinta de enero
   - (C) veinticuatro de diciembre

4. Navidad
   - (A) veinticinco de diciembre
   - (B) veinticuatro de diciembre
   - (C) diecisiete de abril

5. Nochebuena
   - (A) treinta y uno de diciembre
   - (B) uno de enero
   - (C) veinticuatro de diciembre

6. Nochevieja
   - (A) treinta y uno de diciembre
   - (B) uno de enero
   - (C) veinticinco de diciembre

7. Todos los Santos
   - (A) once de noviembre
   - (B) uno de noviembre
   - (C) veintiuno de noviembre

8. Asunción
   - (A) veintiuno de marzo
   - (B) treinta de junio
   - (C) quince de agosto

*Select the correct option for each of these important dates in Spanish history.
More than one answer may be possible.*

1. 19/07/711 : batalla de Guadalete

   Answers page 228

   A) Diecinueve de jullo de setecientos once

   B) Diecinueve de juilio de setecientos once

   C) Diecinueve de julio de setecientos once

2. 12/10/1492 : llegada de Cristóbal Colón a América

   A) Doce de octubre de mil cuatrocientos noventa y dos

   B) Doce de octobre de mil cuatrocientos noventa y dos

   C) Doce de otubre de mil cuatrocientos noventa y dos

3. 06/09/1522 : primera vuelta al mundo por Juan Sebastián Elcano

   A) Seis de septiembre de mil quinientos veintidós

   B) Seis de septembre de mil quinientos veintidós

   C) Seis de setiembre de mil quinientos veintidós

4. 02/05/1808 : levantamiento de Madrid contra Napoleón

   A) Dos de mayo de mil ochocientos ocho

   B) Dos de maio de mil ochocientos ocho

   C) Dos de mallo de mil ochocientos ocho

| **Tema** | **Expressing opinions and preferences** |

Choose the Spanish equivalent of each sentence.

Answers page 228

1. Are you in favour of bullfighting?

   A) ¿Es usted a favor de las corridas de toros?

   B) ¿Es usted en favor de las corridas de toros?

   C) ¿Está usted a favor de las corridas de toros?

   D) ¿Ha usted a favor de las corridas de toros?

2. I am against the government.

   Ⓐ Soy contra el gobierno.

   Ⓑ Estoy en contra del gobierno.

   Ⓒ Soy en contra del gobierno.

   Ⓓ He contra del gobierno.

3. We support speed limits.

   Ⓐ Somos partidarios de limitar la velocidad.

   Ⓑ Estamos partidarios de limitar la velocidad.

   Ⓒ Hemos partidarios de limitar la velocidad.

   Ⓓ Habemos partidarios de limitar la velocidad.

4. You are vegan.

   Ⓐ Habéis veganas.

   Ⓑ Estáis veganas.

   Ⓒ Sois veganas.

5. They are allergic to eggs.

   Ⓐ Son alérgicos a los huevos.

   Ⓑ Han alérgicos a los huevos.

   Ⓒ Están alérgicos a los huevos.

Tema   **Expressing 'getting', 'becoming'**

Choose the appropriate verb to convey the idea of transformation. More than one answer may be possible.

Answers page 228

1. Me ... feliz.

   Ⓐ haces   Ⓑ pones

2. Te has ... muy gordo últimamente.

   Ⓐ hecho   Ⓑ puesto   Ⓒ vuelto

3. Desde que tiene dinero, se ha ... muy antipática.
   - Ⓐ hecho
   - Ⓑ vuelto

4. Con la edad, mis amigos se han ... de derechas.
   - Ⓐ puesto
   - Ⓑ vuelto

5. Todos mis amigos se han ... veganos.
   - Ⓐ hecho
   - Ⓑ puesto
   - Ⓒ vuelto

6. Me he ... alérgico a la carne.
   - Ⓐ hecho
   - Ⓑ puesto
   - Ⓒ vuelto

7. He decidido ... militar.
   - Ⓐ hacerme
   - Ⓑ ponerme
   - Ⓒ volverme

Tema **Remembering and reminding: *recordar* or *acordarse*?**

Select the appropriate verb to complete each sentence. More than one answer may be possible.

Answers page 228

1. Si se le olvida que te debe dinero, ...
   - Ⓐ acuérdaselo.
   - Ⓑ recuérdaselo.

2. No ... nada.
   - Ⓐ acuerdo de
   - Ⓒ me acuerdo de
   - Ⓑ recuerdo
   - Ⓓ me recuerdo de

3. ... tengo cita a las tres, por favor.
   - Ⓐ Acuérdame que
   - Ⓒ Acuérdame de que
   - Ⓑ Recuérdame que
   - Ⓓ Recuérdame de que

4. ... hemos quedado con mis primos.
   - Ⓐ Acuerda que
   - Ⓒ Acuérdate de que
   - Ⓑ Recuerda que
   - Ⓓ Recuérdate de que

5. ¿... aquel viaje a Andalucía?

   Ⓐ Os acordáis de　　　　　Ⓒ Os recordáis

   Ⓑ Acordáis　　　　　　　Ⓓ Os recordáis de

6. ¿No ... lo que me dijiste?

   Ⓐ te acuerdas　　　　　　Ⓒ te recuerdas

   Ⓑ acuerdas de　　　　　　Ⓓ recuerdas

| Tema | **Expressing 'to tell to', 'to say that'** |

Select the translation with the correct meaning in each case.

1. Dice que te olvides de ella.

   Ⓐ She's telling you to forget her.

   Ⓑ She says that you forget her.

Answers page 228

2. Te dice que no te acuerdas del pasado.

   Ⓐ She's telling you not to remember the past.

   Ⓑ She says that you don't remember the past.

3. Dice que no seáis tan de derechas.

   Ⓐ He's telling you not to be so right wing.

   Ⓑ He says that you're not that right wing.

4. Dice que vamos a ver películas en blanco y negro.

   Ⓐ He's telling us to go see black-and-white films.

   Ⓑ He says that we're going to see black-and-white films.

5. Dice que no vayamos a Andalucía.

   Ⓐ He's telling us not to go to Andalucía.

   Ⓑ He says that we're not going to Andalucía.

6. Dice que no creéis en nada.

   Ⓐ He says that you don't believe in anything.

   Ⓑ He's telling you not to believe in anything.

Choose the correct verb form to complete each sentence.

1. La madre le dice a su hijo que ... prudente con la moto.

   Ⓐ es   Ⓑ sea

2. Le dice que no ... muy rápido.

   Ⓐ va   Ⓑ vaya

3. El hijo le dice que no ...

   Ⓐ se preocupa.   Ⓑ se preocupe.

4. Le dice que él siempre ... con prudencia.

   Ⓐ conduce   Ⓑ conduzca

5. Le dice a su madre que ... tranquila.

   Ⓐ está   Ⓑ esté

6. Le dice que ... dormir tranquila.

   Ⓐ puede   Ⓑ pueda

Tema **The preterite (irregular forms)**

Indicate if the correct preterite form is used or not.

Answers
page 228

1. No tuve tiempo de llamarte, disculpa.

   Ⓐ Yes   Ⓑ No

2. ¿Hubo gente?

   Ⓐ Yes   Ⓑ No

3. Tuvo muchos invitados para Nochevieja.

   Ⓐ Yes   Ⓑ No

4. Hubieron un compromiso y no pudieron venir.

   Ⓐ Yes   Ⓑ No

5. Tuvieron que irse a un hotel.

   Ⓐ Yes   Ⓑ No

6. Aunque soy vegano, hube que comer carne.

    Ⓐ Yes   Ⓑ No

7. ¿No hubiste hambre?

    Ⓐ Yes   Ⓑ No

Choose the correct preterite form to change each sentence to the past. **Answers page 228**

1. Este año vienen mis padres a celebrar Nochebuena.

    Ⓐ veneron   Ⓑ vineron   Ⓒ vinieron   Ⓓ venieron

2. También viene un compañero de la oficina.

    Ⓐ vino   Ⓑ vine   Ⓒ vinió   Ⓓ vinó

3. Vengo para el postre.

    Ⓐ vino   Ⓑ vine   Ⓒ vinó   Ⓓ viné

4. No puedo probar la carne.

    Ⓐ pudé   Ⓑ pudo   Ⓒ podí   Ⓓ pude

5. No pueden quedarse para las doce uvas.

    Ⓐ puderon   Ⓑ poderon   Ⓒ podieron   Ⓓ pudieron

6. ¿Nadie puede ayudarte?

    Ⓐ pudo   Ⓑ pude   Ⓒ pudió   Ⓓ pudó

Expressing opinions   ÚTILES

ser partidario/a de	*to be in favour of* (m./f.)
estar a favor de	*to be for*
estar en contra de	*to be against*
ser de derechas	*to be right wing*
ser de izquierdas	*to be left wing*

What day is it?

¿Qué día es hoy?	*What day is it today?*
Es + **(lunes, martes**, etc.**)**	*It's (Monday, Tuesday, etc.)*
¿A qué día estamos?	*What day is it?*
Estamos a + **(miércoles, jueves**, etc.**)**	*It's (Wednesday, Thursday, etc.)*

Months of the year

enero	*January*
febrero	*February*
marzo	*March*
abril	*April*
mayo	*May*
junio	*June*
julio	*July*
agosto	*August*
septiembre/setiembre	*September*
octubre	*October*
noviembre	*November*
diciembre	*December*

Some holidays

Día de los Inocentes	*April Fool's Day*
Día de Reyes	*Epiphany (Three Kings' Day)*
Navidad	*Christmas*
Nochebuena	*Christmas Eve*
Nochevieja	*New Year's Eve*
Todos los Santos	*All Saints' Day*

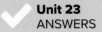

Unit 23
ANSWERS

PAGE 219

What day is it?

1 **B** 2 **A** 3 **C** 4 **A** 5 **A** 6 **A** 7 **B** 8 **C, D**

1 **B** 2 **B** 3 **A** 4 **A** 5 **C** 6 **A** 7 **B** 8 **C**

1 **C** 2 **A** 3 **A** **C** 4 **A**

PAGE 221

Expressing opinions and preferences

1 **C** 2 **B** 3 **A** 4 **C** 5 **A**

PAGE 222

Expressing 'getting', 'becoming'

1 **A** 2 **B** 3 **B** 4 **B** 5 **A, C** 6 **C** 7 **A, C**

PAGE 223

Remembering and reminding: *recordar* or *acordarse*?

1 **B** 2 **B, C** 3 **B** 4 **B, C** 5 **A** 6 **D**

PAGE 224

Expressing 'to tell to', 'to say that'

1 **A** 2 **B** 3 **A** 4 **B** 5 **A** 6 **A**

1 **B** 2 **B** 3 **B** 4 **A** 5 **B** 6 **A**

PAGE 225

The preterite (irregular forms)

1 **A** 2 **A** 3 **A** 4 **B** 5 **A** 6 **B** 7 **B**

1 **C** 2 **A** 3 **B** 4 **D** 5 **D** 6 **A**

YOUR SCORE:

Did you get between 0 and 12? ¡Ay, ay, ay!

Did you get between 13 and 25? Muy justito...

Did you get between 26 and 38? No está mal, pero...

Did you get between 39 and 51? Enhorabuena.

Did you get 52 or over? ¡Eres un auténtico fenómeno!

Tema **Cuts of meat**

Select the type of meat that corresponds to the cut. More than one answer may be possible.

Answers page 238

1. un ala de...
   - Ⓐ conejo
   - Ⓑ pollo
   - Ⓒ ternera

2. una pechuga de...
   - Ⓐ pollo
   - Ⓑ conejo
   - Ⓒ pavo

3. un filete de...
   - Ⓐ ternera
   - Ⓑ conejo
   - Ⓒ buey

4. una chuleta de...
   - Ⓐ pavo
   - Ⓑ cordero
   - Ⓒ cerdo

5. un chuletón de...
   - Ⓐ buey
   - Ⓑ ternera
   - Ⓒ conejo

6. un muslo de...
   - Ⓐ pavo
   - Ⓑ pollo
   - Ⓒ gallo

7. un solomillo de...
   - Ⓐ cerdo
   - Ⓑ gallo
   - Ⓒ ternera

Tema **Types of food**

Choose the category each of these foods belongs to.

Answers page 238

1. el lenguado
   - Ⓐ aves
   - Ⓑ embutidos
   - Ⓒ mariscos
   - Ⓓ pescados

2. la codorniz
   - Ⓐ aves
   - Ⓑ embutidos
   - Ⓒ mariscos
   - Ⓓ pescados

3. el pato
   - Ⓐ aves
   - Ⓑ embutidos
   - Ⓒ mariscos
   - Ⓓ pescados

4. la cigala
   - Ⓐ aves
   - Ⓑ embutidos
   - Ⓒ mariscos
   - Ⓓ pescados

5. la morcilla
  - A aves
  - B embutidos
  - C mariscos
  - D pescados

6. la gallina
  - A aves
  - B embutidos
  - C mariscos
  - D pescados

7. el atún
  - A aves
  - B embutidos
  - C mariscos
  - D pescados

8. la salchicha
  - A aves
  - B embutidos
  - C mariscos
  - D pescados

9. la almeja
  - A aves
  - B embutidos
  - C mariscos
  - D pescados

10. la ostra
  - A aves
  - B embutidos
  - C mariscos
  - D pescados

11. el bacalao
  - A aves
  - B embutidos
  - C mariscos
  - D pescados

12. el chorizo
  - A aves
  - B embutidos
  - C mariscos
  - D pescados

Tema **At the restaurant (1)**

Choose the correct option in each case. More than one may be possible.

Answers page 238

1. Quisiera ... de agua.
  - A un vaso
  - B una jarra
  - C un jarrón

2. ¿La quiere fría o ... ?
  - A al tiempo
  - B del tiempo
  - C con tiempo

3. El agua, ¿... o ... ?
  - A con gas / sin gas
  - B con el gas / sin el gas
  - C con gaseosa / sin gaseosa

4 La carne, ... por favor.

A a punto   B al punto   C del punto

5 ¿Qué ... tiene?

A garnitura   B guarnición   C acompañamiento

6 De postre, una tarta ...

A a la fresa.   B de fresa.   C a fresa.

7 ... aproveche.

A Que   B Vaya   C Buen

Tema Tapas

Select the correct description for each of these tapas.

Answers
page 238

1. boquerones

A anchovies   B meatballs

2. albóndigas

A meatballs   B cod fritters

3. gambas con gabardina

A boiled shrimp   B shrimp tempura

4. patatas bravas

A potato nuggets   B cubed, fried potatoes served with a spicy sauce

5. ensaladilla

A a green salad   B a Russian salad

6. callos

A tripe   B quail

7. pinchitos

A cuttlefish   B brochettes

| Tema | At the restaurant (2) |

Choose the correct order for each exchange.

1.

A. ¿A nombre de quién?

B   He reservado una mesa para dos personas.

C   Juan Córdoba

Answers page 238

- Ⓐ C – B – A
- Ⓑ A – C – B
- Ⓒ B – A – C

2.

A   ¿Dónde está el servicio, por favor?

B   ¿Está buscando algo?

C   La segunda puerta al fondo.

- Ⓐ A – B – C
- Ⓑ B – C – A
- Ⓒ B – A – C

3.

A   De momento no hay, son quince minutos de espera.

B   Lo siento, tenemos prisa.

C   Queríamos una mesa fuera, al fresco.

- Ⓐ C – B – A
- Ⓑ B – C – A
- Ⓒ C – A – B

4.

A   ¿Cómo quiere el chuletón?

B   Ni demasiado crudo ni pasado.

C   Término medio entonces.

- Ⓐ C – A – B
- Ⓑ A – B – C
- Ⓒ A – C – B

Tema	**The -ing form of the verb**

Select the correct -ing form of the verb in each case.

Answers page 238

1. ... la tele se pierde mucho tiempo.
   - A Veyendo
   - B Viendo
   - C Vendo

2. ... libros se aprenden más cosas.
   - A Leyendo
   - B Legendo
   - C Liendo

3. Te estoy ... ayuda.
   - A pediendo
   - B piedendo
   - C pidiendo

4. ... hacerlo, ¿por qué no lo haces?
   - A Puediendo
   - B Pudiendo
   - C Podiendo

5. ... no vas a conseguir nada.
   - A Durmiendo
   - B Duermiendo
   - C Dormiendo

Select the correctly constructed sentence. More than one answer may be possible.

1. We are telling them about our vacation.
   - A Les estamos contando nuestras vacaciones.
   - B Estamos les contando nuestras vacaciones.
   - C Estamos contándoles nuestras vacaciones.

Answers page 238

2. He is putting on weight.
   - A Está se poniendo gordo.
   - C Está poniéndose gordo.
   - B Se está poniendo gordo.

3. That's what I'm telling you.
   - A Te lo estoy diciendo.
   - C Te estoy lo diciendo.
   - B Estoy diciéndotelo.
   - D Estoy te lo diciendo.

4. We are reminding them about that.
   - A Estamos se lo recordando.
   - C Estamos recordándoselo.
   - B Se lo estamos recordando.
   - D Estamos se recordándolo.

| Tema | Noun-article-adjective agreement |

Choose the option that agrees with the noun in gender and number.

Answers page 238

1. Me sienta mal ... agua ...
   - A la / fría
   - B el / fría
   - C el / frío
   - D la / frío

2. ... aguas minerales no siempre son ....
   - A Los / buenos
   - B Las / buenas
   - C Los / buenas
   - D Las / buenos

3. No es ... ... agua que ... que tomé ayer.
   - A la misma / la
   - B el mismo / el
   - C el mismo / la
   - D la misma / el

4. Me gustan ... aves ...
   - A los / blancos
   - B los / blancas
   - C las / blancos
   - D las / blancas

5. Soy alérgico a ... aves.
   - A todas las
   - B todos los
   - C todas los
   - D todos las

6. ... ave es más ... que la ternera.
   - A La / tierna
   - B La / tierno
   - C El / tierna
   - D El / tierno

| Tema | The future tense |

Answers page 238

Choose the correct future form of the verb to complete each sentence.

1. Siempre pido carne, pero hoy... pescado.
   - A pidiró
   - B pediré
   - C pediró
   - D pidiré

2. Son veganos y siempre lo ...
   - A serón.
   - B serán.
   - C erán.
   - D serén.

3. Si no vamos al restaurante hoy, ... otro día.

   Ⓐ varemos   Ⓑ veremos   Ⓒ iremos   Ⓓ iramos

4. Si no estáis satisfechos, es que no lo ... nunca.

   Ⓐ estaréis   Ⓑ estaráis   Ⓒ estarás   Ⓓ estarés

5. Si no duermes ahora, ... mañana.

   Ⓐ duermirás   Ⓑ duermerás   Ⓒ dormerás   Ⓓ dormirás

6. Si no aprueba el carné este año, lo ... el que viene.

   Ⓐ apruebará   Ⓑ apruebará   Ⓒ aprobará   Ⓓ aproberá

Choose the most suitable verb for each context.

1. ¿Crees que ... mucha gente?

   Ⓐ habrá   Ⓑ hará

   Answers page 238

2. ¿Crees que ... tiempo para cenar?

   Ⓐ habrá   Ⓑ hará

3. ¿Crees que ... buen tiempo?

   Ⓐ habrá   Ⓑ hará

4. Mañana ... un año que estamos casados.

   Ⓐ habrá   Ⓑ hará

5. Mi mujer nunca ... las lentejas como las hacía mi madre.

   Ⓐ habrá   Ⓑ hará

6. Si llegamos tarde ... que esperar.

   Ⓐ habrá   Ⓑ hará

7. Si llegamos tarde ... falta esperar.

   Ⓐ habrá   Ⓑ hará

8. No ... falta que me ayudes, gracias.

   Ⓐ habrá   Ⓑ hará

Verbs

aprovechar	*to take advantage of, to enjoy* (**Que aproveche.** or **Buen provecho.** *Enjoy your meal!*)
sentar mal	*to not go down well* (a remark, a food, etc.) (verb with a spelling change)

Cuts of meat

el ala (f.)	*wing*
la chuleta	*chop*
el chuletón	*T-bone steak*
el filete	*steak, fillet*
el muslo	*thigh*
la pechuga	*breast*
el solomillo	*sirloin steak*

Fresh and cured meats

el buey	*beef* (in Spain, beef from an ox over the age of four)
el cerdo	*pork*
el chorizo	*chorizo* (spicy pork sausage)
el conejo	*rabbit*
el cordero	*lamb*
los embutidos	*cold cuts, cured meats*
la morcilla	*black pudding, blood sausage*
la salchicha	*sausage*
la ternera	*veal* (in Spain, beef from a calf between the age of 8 and 12 months)

Poultry

el ave (f.)	*poultry*
la codorniz	*quail*

la gallina	hen
el gallo	cock
el pato	duck
el pavo	turkey
el pollo	chicken

Fish and seafood

la almeja	clam
el atún	tuna
el bacalao	cod
la cigala	Dublin Bay prawn, Norway lobster, scampi, langoustine
el lenguado	sole
la ostra	oyster

Water

la jarra	carafe (**el jarrón** vase)
el agua (f.)	water
agua con gas / sin gas	sparkling water / non-carbonated water
del tiempo	at room temperature
frío/a	cold (m./f.)

Ordering a meat dish

al punto	medium rare (or **término medio**)
crudo/a	raw (m./f.)
muy hecho/a	well done (m./f.)
pasado/a	overcooked (m./f.)
poco hecho/a	rare (m./f.)
la guarnición	garnish, side dish
el acompañamiento	side dish

ESENCIALES

PAGE 229
Cuts of meat
1 **B** 2 **A**, **C** 3 **A**, **C** 4 **B**, **C** 5 **A**, **B** 6 **A**, **B**, **C** 7 **A**, **C**

Types of food
1 **D** 2 **A** 3 **A** 4 **C** 5 **B** 6 **A** 7 **D** 8 **B** 9 **C** 10 **C** 11 **D** 12 **B**

PAGE 230
At the restaurant (1)
1 **A**, **B** 2 **B** 3 **A** 4 **B** 5 **B**, **C** 6 **B** 7 **A**

PAGE 231
Tapas
1 **A** 2 **A** 3 **B** 4 **B** 5 **B** 6 **A** 7 **B**

PAGE 232
At the restaurant (2)
1 **C** 2 **C** 3 **C** 4 **B**

PAGE 233
The -ing form of the verb
1 **B** 2 **A** 3 **C** 4 **B** 5 **A**
1 **A**, **C** 2 **B**, **C** 3 **A**, **B** 4 **B**, **C**

PAGE 234
Noun-article-adjective agreement
1 **B** 2 **B** 3 **A** 4 **D** 5 **A** 6 **C**

The future tense
1 **B** 2 **B** 3 **C** 4 **A** 5 **D** 6 **C**
1 **A** 2 **A** 3 **B** 4 **B** 5 **B** 6 **A** 7 **B** 8 **B**

YOUR
SCORE:

Did you get between 0 and 12? ¡Ay, ay, ay!

Did you get between 13 and 25? Muy justito...

Did you get between 26 and 38? No está mal, pero...

Did you get between 39 and 51? Enhorabuena.

Did you get 52 or over? ¡Eres un auténtico fenómeno!

| Tema | **The seasons** |

Select the correct option to complete the name of the season.

Answers
page 249

1. Las hojas de los árboles caen al suelo en oto...

   A ...no.   **B** ...ño.   **C** ...na.   **D** ...ña.

2. Voy a esquiar a Sierra Nevada en ...vierno.

   A hi...   **B** hin...   **C** i...   **D** in...

3. Siempre me pongo muy morena en ve...

   A ...roño.   **B** ...rano.   **C** ...raño.   **D** ...rono.

4. La naturaleza renace en ...vera.

   A prima...   **B** primo...   **C** premi...   **D** prema...

Choose the sentence with the appropriate term for 'season' in each case.

Answers
page 249

1. I love *The Four Seasons* by Vivaldi.

   A Me encantan *Las cuatro temporadas* de Vivaldi.

   B Me encantan *Las cuatro estaciones* de Vivaldi.

2. I only eat fruit that is in season.

   A Solo como fruta de temporada.

   B Solo como fruta de estación.

3. This season everyone is wearing yellow.

   A Esta temporada se llevará el amarillo.

   B Esta estación se llevará el amarillo.

4. The theatre season begins in September.

   A La temporada teatral comienza en septiembre.

   B La estación teatral comienza en septiembre.

5. He never wears seasonal colours.

   A Nunca lleva colores de temporada.

   B Nunca lleva colores de estación.

6. The seasons are opposite in the two hemispheres.

　A　Las temporadas están invertidas entre los dos hemisferios.

　B　Las estaciones están invertidas entre los dos hemisferios.

Tema **Clothing size and fit**

Choose the most appropriate word to complete each sentence. More than one answer may be possible.

Answers page 249

1. ¿Qué talla ... usted?

　A　usa　　　B　gasta　　　C　queda　　　D　hace

2. Este pantalón me queda un poco estrecho de...

　A　hombros.　　B　cintura.　　C　cinturón.　　D　codos.

3. Y esta chaqueta me queda larga de ...

　A　hombros.　　B　cintura.　　C　mangas.　　D　codos.

4. Si le queda ancho, hacemos ...

　A　arreglos.　　B　secciones.　　C　regalos.　　D　gangas.

5. Las minifaldas te ...

　A　sientan bien.　　B　quedan bien.　　C　favorecen.　　D　prueban.

Tema **At the clothing store**

Select the most appropriate verb for each context. More than one answer may be possible.

Answers page 249

1. Buenas, me han regalado esta falda y quiero ...

　A　probármela.　　　　C　devolverla.

　B　cambiarla.　　　　D　ponérmela.

2. Cambiamos los artículos pero no ... el dinero.

　A　cambiamos　　　　C　volvemos

　B　devolvemos　　　　D　regalamos

3. Si ha ... el tique, no aceptamos devoluciones.

   A perdido   C comprado

   B tirado   D cambiado

4. Está baratísimo, es una auténtica...

   A ropa.   C ganga.

   B falda.   D talla.

5. Es un poco caro, esperaré ...

   A las rebajas.   C las soldas.

   B los rebajos.   D los soldados.

Tema **To wait (*esperar*) or to serve (*atender*)?**

Select the correct verb in each case.

Answers page 249

1. ... a que haga frío para sacar el abrigo.

   A Atenderé   B Esperaré

2. En esta tienda el personal ... muy bien al cliente.

   A atiende   B espera

3. Buenos días, le ... Marta, ¿en qué puedo ayudarle?

   A atiende   B espera

4. Cuando llegas el último, siempre hay que ...

   A atender.   B esperar.

5. ..., llego enseguida.

   A Atiéndeme   B Espérame

6. Estoy buscando al dependiente que me ... ayer.

   A atendió   B esperó

Unit 25
ESENCIALES

Choose the correct option to complete each sentence.

1. Está prohibido ...

   Ⓐ fumar.　　　　Ⓑ de fumar.

Answers page 249

2. Es difícil ... un buen regalo.

   Ⓐ elegir　　　　Ⓑ de elegir

3. Esta clienta es difícil ...

   Ⓐ satisfacer.　　　　Ⓑ de satisfacer.

4. Es imprescindible ... la ropa antes de comprarla.

   Ⓐ probarse　　　　Ⓑ de probarse

5. Me gusta la ropa sencilla y fácil ...

   Ⓐ conjuntar.　　　　Ⓑ de conjuntar.

6. Es un problema ... un 47 de pie.

   Ⓐ gastar　　　　Ⓑ de gastar

7. Cuesta caro ... la moda.

   Ⓐ seguir　　　　Ⓑ de seguir

8. Algunas modas son difíciles ...

   Ⓐ seguir.　　　　Ⓑ de seguir.

9. El amarillo es un color difícil ...

   Ⓐ llevar.　　　　Ⓑ de llevar.

10. Es difícil ... una prenda amarilla y que te siente bien.

    Ⓐ llevar　　　　Ⓑ de llevar

11. ¿Es posible ... tanto en ropa?

    Ⓐ gastar　　　　Ⓑ de gastar

12. Lo que quiere este cliente es ... entender.

    Ⓐ imposible　　　　Ⓑ imposible de

Tema **Negative sentences**

Select the correct construction for each sentence. More than one may be possible.

1. I never wear miniskirts.

   Ⓐ Nunca me pongo minifaldas.

   Ⓑ No me pongo nunca minifaldas.

   Ⓒ Nunca no me pongo minifaldas.

   Ⓓ Me pongo nunca minifaldas.

Answers page 249

2. Yellow doesn't suit anyone.

   Ⓐ A nadie no le sienta bien el amarillo.

   Ⓑ A nadie le sienta bien el amarillo.

   Ⓒ No le sienta bien a nadie el amarillo.

   Ⓓ Le sienta bien a nadie el amarillo.

3. You never give me anything.

   Ⓐ Nunca no me regalas nada.

   Ⓑ No me regalas nunca nada.

   Ⓒ Nada no me regalas nunca.

   Ⓓ Nunca me regalas nada.

4. I don't like going shopping either.

   Ⓐ Tampoco me gusta ir de tiendas.

   Ⓑ Tampoco no me gusta ir de tiendas.

   Ⓒ No me gusta tampoco ir de tiendas.

   Ⓓ Me gusta tampoco ir de tiendas.

5. They don't even have a men's section.

   Ⓐ No tienen ni siquiera sección de caballeros.

   Ⓑ Ni siquiera no tienen sección de caballeros.

   Ⓒ Tienen ni siquiera sección de caballeros.

   Ⓓ Ni siquiera tienen sección de caballeros.

6. He doesn't even know his shoe size.

   (A) Ni sabe qué pie gasta.

   (B) No sabe ni qué pie gasta.

   (C) Sabe ni qué pie gasta.

   (D) Ni no sabe qué pie gasta.

Tema **Tense sequence with *con tal de que* (so long as)**

*Choose the correct option with the main clause in the future tense and the subordinate clause (introduced by **con tal de que**) in the subjunctive.*

1. Te devuelvo el dinero si tienes el tique.

Answers page 249

   (A) Te devuelveré el dinero con tal de que tienas el tique.

   (B) Te devolveré el dinero con tal de que tengas el tique.

   (C) Te devolvré el dinero con tal de que tendrás el tique.

   (D) Te devuelvaré el dinero con tal de que tiengas el tique.

2. Podemos comprar estos zapatos si nos haces un descuento.

   (A) Poderemos comprar estos zapatos con tal de que nos hagues un descuento.

   (B) Podramos comprar estos zapatos con tal de que nos hagas un descuento.

   (C) Poderamos comprar estos zapatos con tal de que nos harás un descuento.

   (D) Podremos comprar estos zapatos con tal de que nos hagas un descuento.

3. Este pantalón te queda bien si te pones un cinturón.

   (A) Este pantalón te quedrá bien con tal de que te pongues un cinturón.

   (B) Este pantalón te quedré bien con tal de que te ponias un cinturón.

   (C) Este pantalón te quede bien con tal de que te pondrás un cinturón.

   (D) Este pantalón te quedará bien con tal de que te pongas un cinturón.

4. Se ponen una corbata si vosotras os ponéis un vestido.

   A Se podrán una corbata con tal de que vosotras os ponguéis un vestido.

   B Se ponrán una corbata con tal de que vosotras os pondráis un vestido.

   C Se pondrán una corbata con tal de que vosotras os pongáis un vestido.

   D Se ponerán una corbata con tal de que vosotras os pondréis un vestido.

Tema **Tense sequence with *aunque* (even if)**

*Choose the correct pair of verbs, with the main clause in the future tense and the subordinate clause (introduced by **aunque**) in the subjunctive.*

1. Aunque me lo ..., no lo ...

   Answers page 249

   A regales / queré.

   C regalas / querró.

   B regales / querré.

   D regalas / quereré.

---

2. Aunque ... rebajado, nunca ... bastante dinero para comprarlo.

   A esté / tendréis

   C está / tendráis

   B esté / teneréis

   D sea / teneráis

---

3. ... ir de tiendas con él, aunque no te ...

   A Deberás / apetezca.

   C deberás / apetezque.

   B Debrás / apetezca.

   D debrás / apetezque.

---

4. Siempre ... el amarillo, aunque les ... mal ese color.

   A elegerán / sienta

   C eligirán / sienta

   B eligerán / siente

   D elegirán / siente

---

5. No me ... esa falda, aunque me lo ...

   A podré / pides.

   C pondré / pidas.

   B poneré / pidas.

   D poderé / pides.

Unit 25
ESENCIALES

Select the correct translation for each sentence.

1. Yellow is in fashion.

    (A) El amarillo es de moda.

    (B) El amarillo es a la moda.

    (C) El amarillo está de moda.

    (D) El amarillo está a la moda.

Answers page 249

2. This shirt doesn't suit you at all.

    (A) Esta camisa te queda fatal.

    (B) Esta camisa te quedas fatal.

    (C) Esta camisa se te quedas fatal.

    (D) Esta camisa quedas fatal.

3. Between the sport coat and the pullover, I'll take the pullover.

    (A) Entre la americana y el jersey, quedo el jersey.

    (B) Entre la americana y el jersey, quedo con el jersey.

    (C) Entre la americana y el jersey, me queda con el jersey.

    (D) Entre la americana y el jersey, me quedo con el jersey.

4. These clothes are not in good shape.

    (A) Estas ropas no están en buen estado.

    (B) Estos ropas no están en buen estado.

    (C) Esta ropa no está en buen estado.

    (D) Este ropa no está en buen estado.

Verbs   ÚTILES

atender	*to look after, to attend to, to serve*
cambiar	*to change, to exchange*
comenzar	*to begin* (verb with a spelling change)

conjuntar	*to combine, to match, to coordinate*
deber	*to owe*
esperar	*to wait, to hope*
esquiar	*to ski*
estar de moda	*to be in fashion*
favorecer	*to favour, to support*
gastar	*to take (a size)* **¿Qué pie gasta?** *What is your shoe size?*
probarse	*to try on clothes* (verb with a spelling change)
quedar bien / mal	*to suit, to fit / to not suit, to not fit* (clothing)
quedarse con	*to take an item*
renacer	*to be reborn, to revive*
satisfacer	*to satisfy*
tirar	*to throw away*
usar	*to wear, to take (a size)*

Seasons

la estación	*season* (of the year)
la temporada	*season* (other periods)
la primavera	*spring*
el verano	*summer*
el otoño	*autumn*
el invierno	*winter*

Clothing

el abrigo	*overcoat*
la cintura	*waist*
el cinturón	*belt*

el codo	*elbow*
la corbata	*necktie*
el hombro	*shoulder*
la manga	*sleeve*
la minifalda	*miniskirt*
la prenda	*item of clothing, garment*
la talla	*size*

Buying clothes

el arreglo	*alteration*
la sección	*section, department*
la ganga	*bargain*
el artículo	*article*
el tique	*receipt*
la devolución	*refund*
el descuento	*discount*
las rebajas	*sales*

Adjectives

ancho/a	*loose, baggy* (m./f.)
difícil	*difficult*
estrecho/a	*tight, small* (m./f.)
fácil	*easy*
imprescindible	*indispensable, essential*
prohibido/a	*forbidden* (m./f.)
rebajado/a	*discounted* (m./f.)
sencillo/a	*simple, plain* (m./f.)

ESENCIALES

PAGE 239
The seasons
1 B 2 D 3 B 4 A
1 B 2 A 3 A 4 A 5 A 6 B

. . . .

PAGE 240
Clothes size and fit
1 A, B 2 A, B 3 C 4 A 5 A, B, C

At the clothes shop
1 B C 2 B 3 A B 4 C 5 A

. . . .

PAGE 241
To wait (*esperar*) or to serve (*atender*)?
1 B 2 A 3 A 4 B 5 B 6 A

. . . .

PAGE 242
The preposition *de*
1 A 2 A 3 B 4 A 5 B 6 A 7 A 8 B 9 B 10 A 11 A 12 B

. . . .

PAGE 243
Negative sentences
1 A, B 2 B, C 3 B, D 4 A, C 5 A, D 6 A, B

. . . .

PAGE 244
Tense sequence with *con tal de que* (so long as)
1 B 2 D 3 D 4 C

. . . .

PAGE 245
Tense sequence with *aunque* (even if)
1 B 2 A 3 A 4 D 5 C

. . . .

PAGE 246
Translation
1 C 2 A 3 D 4 C

YOUR SCORE:

Did you get between 0 and 10? ¡Ay, ay, ay!

Did you get between 11 and 21? Muy justito...

Did you get between 22 and 32? No está mal, pero...

Did you get between 33 and 43? Enhorabuena.

Did you get 44 or over? ¡Eres un auténtico fenómeno!

Unit 26
ESENCIALES

Answers page 259

Tema Size and weight

Select the correct option for each measurement.

1. Mido 2 m y peso 100 k.

   A dos metres / cientos kilos   C dos metros / cien kilos

   B dos metras / ciento kilos

2. El colibrí mide entre 9 y 15 cm.

   A nueve y quince centímetras   C nueve y quince centímetres

   B nueve y quince centímetros

3. Pesa entre 5 y 8 g.

   A cinco y ocho gramos   C cinco y ocho gramas

   B cinco y ocho grames

4. Un elefante adulto puede pesar más de 7 T.

   A siete toneladas   C siete tonelades

   B siete tonelados

Answers page 259

Tema Fractions, decimals, percentages and proportions

Select the correct option for each measurement or figure. More than one answer may be possible.

1. Necesito 1,5 l de leche.

   A una litra y media   B uno litro y medio   C un litro y medio

2. Quiero ¼ k de jamón.

   A un cuarto de kilo   B una cuarta de kilo   C un cuarte de kilo

3. Dame ½ k de carne.

   A un medio kilo   B medio un kilo   C medio kilo

4. El valor de pi es 3,14.

   A tres coma catorce   B tres como catorce   C tres come catorce

5. Hay un 30% de abstenciones.

   Ⓐ treinta por cientas   Ⓑ treinta por ciento   Ⓒ treinta por cientos

6. ½ españoles nunca hace ejercicio.

   Ⓐ La mitad de los   Ⓑ Uno de cada dos   Ⓒ El medio de los

7. 1/5 españoles no come carne.

   Ⓐ La quinta parte   Ⓑ Uno sobre los   Ⓒ Uno sobre cinco
   de los   cinco

8. 2/3 españoles prefieren el horario de verano.

   Ⓐ Las dos terceras   Ⓑ Las dos tercias   Ⓒ Dos de cada tres
   partes de los   partes de los

Tema IT vocabulary

Choose the Spanish word that corresponds to each IT term. More than one answer may be correct.

1. laptop computer

   Ⓐ portable   Ⓑ portátil   Ⓒ móvil

2. Internet search

   Ⓐ búsqueda   Ⓑ busca   Ⓒ búsquedad

3. screen

   Ⓐ escritorio   Ⓑ pantalla   Ⓒ cargador

4. wireless

   Ⓐ móvil   Ⓑ portátil   Ⓒ inalámbrico

5. USB flash drive

   Ⓐ lápiz   Ⓑ pincho   Ⓒ pen

6. mouse

   Ⓐ rata   Ⓑ ratón   Ⓒ sonrisa

Answers page 259

Unit 26
ESENCIALES

Choose the most appropriate word to complete each sentence. More than one answer may be possible.

Answers page 259

1. No sé si comprarme un portátil o un ordenador de ...

   (A) escritorio.　　(B) sobremesa.　　(C) meseta.

2. La información está en el ... adjunto.

   (A) fichero　　(B) archivo　　(C) teclado

3. Tienes demasiados documentos abiertos, organízalos en ...

   (A) respaldos.　　(B) carpetas.　　(C) dorsales.

4. ... en este icono.

   (A) Pincha　　(B) Haz clic　　(C) Haz clac

5. Te mando un ... interesante.

   (A) lazo　　(B) enlace　　(C) vínculo

6. ¿Me das la ... de tu correo electrónico, cariño?

   (A) contraseña　　(B) señal　　(C) tecla

Select the correct verb to complete each phrase. More than one answer may be possible.

Answers page 25

1. Mi abuela tiene noventa años, pero ... perfectamente en Internet.

   (A) almacena　　(B) cuelga　　(C) descarga

   (D) enchufa　　(E) navega　　(F) se queda colgado

2. Este disco duro ... horas de música.

   (A) almacena　　(B) cuelga　　(C) descarga

   (D) enchufa　　(E) navega　　(F) se queda colgado

3. La batería es antigua y se ... enseguida.

   (A) almacena　　(B) cuelga　　(C) descarga

   (D) enchufa　　(E) navega　　(F) se queda colgado

4. ... el ordenador y deja que la batería cargue al 100%.

   Ⓐ Almacena   Ⓑ Cuelga   Ⓒ Descarga

   Ⓓ Enchufa   Ⓔ Navega   Ⓕ Se queda colgado

5. Mi ordenador tiene un virus y ... a cada rato.

   Ⓐ almacena   Ⓑ cuelga   Ⓒ descarga

   Ⓓ enchufa   Ⓔ navega   Ⓕ se queda colgado

6. Mi primo es un loco de cine: ... decenas de películas cada día.

   Ⓐ almacena   Ⓑ cuelga   Ⓒ descarga

   Ⓓ enchufa   Ⓔ navega   Ⓕ se queda colgado

Tema   **Relative pronouns**

Choose the correct relative pronoun to complete each sentence. Both might be possible in some cases.

1. Esta es la tienda ... he comprado mi ordenador.

   Ⓐ donde   Ⓑ en que

   Answers page 259

2. No me acuerdo de la carpeta ... he metido la foto.

   Ⓐ donde   Ⓑ en que

3. Hubo un tiempo ... nadie tenía ordenadores.

   Ⓐ donde   Ⓑ en que

4. La casa ... nací existe todavía.

   Ⓐ donde   Ⓑ en que

5. ¿Te acuerdas del día ... el hombre llegó a la Luna?

   Ⓐ donde   Ⓑ en que

6. He borrado el archivo ... había apuntado esos datos.

   Ⓐ donde   Ⓑ en que

7. Tu vida cambia a partir del momento ... tienes un ordenador.

   Ⓐ donde   Ⓑ en que

8. Este será el siglo ... la tecnología cambió el mundo.

   A donde   **B** en que

9. Enero es el mes ... la gente está más deprimida.

   A donde   **B** en que

10. El único sitio ... descanso es en el campo, sin conexión.

    A donde   **B** en que

Tema **Any, whichever, anyone, any old, etc.**

Choose the correct masculine or feminine form for each context.

Answers page 259

1. Arreglar un ordenador no lo puede hacer ...

   A cualquier.   **B** cualquiera.

2. Si tienes ... duda, llámame.

   A cualquier   **B** cualquiera

3. Para ... problema, puede llamar a la asistencia en línea.

   A cualquier   **B** cualquiera

4. No pienso comprarlo a ... precio.

   A cualquier   **B** cualquiera

5. No es un dispositivo ..., por eso es caro.

   A cualquier   **B** cualquiera

6. No me importa el modelo: para lo que hago, ... me sirve.

   A cualquier   **B** cualquiera

7. Sin un buen antivirus, ... día vas a tener problemas.

   A cualquier   **B** cualquiera

8. No tengo preferencia: ... de los dos.

   A cualquier   **B** cualquiera

Tema	Talking about the future

The sentences provided are in the near future (ir + a + infinitive). For each, choose the option that uses the future tense to express a more distant future.

Answers page 259

1. Va a hacer frío hoy.   Mañana ...
   - A habrá frío.
   - B hará frío.
   - C hacerá frío.

2. ¿Vas a poder venir esta tarde?   Pasado mañana, ...
   - A ¿podrás venir?
   - B ¿podrés venir?
   - C ¿poderás venir?

3. No te lo voy a decir ahora.   La semana que viene ...
   - A te lo diró.
   - B te lo deciró.
   - C te lo diré.

4. Enseguida van a venir.   El jueves próximo ...
   - A vendrán.
   - B venerán.
   - C viendrán.

5. Vamos a saberlo a las once.   Pronto...
   - A lo saberemos.
   - B lo sabremos.
   - C lo sabramos.

6. Os va a gustar.   Un día ...
   - A os gustaréis.
   - B os gustará.
   - C os gustaréis.

Tema	Tense sequence in the future

Select the pair of verbs that convey a possible action in the future (the future tense in the main clause and the subjunctive in the subordinate clause).

Answers page 259

1. Cuando ... rico, ... una tele de 98 pulgadas.
   - A seré / compraré
   - C seré / compre
   - B sea / compre
   - D sea / compraré

2. ¿Me ... llamar en cuanto ... en casa?
   - A podáis / estéis
   - C podáis / estaréis
   - B podréis / estéis
   - D podréis / estaréis

3. ... esa película el día en que ... tiempo.
   - A Veremos / tendremos
   - C Veremos / tengamos
   - B Veamos / tendremos
   - D Veamos / tengamos

4. Te ... moreno en cuanto ... unos días a la playa.

- **A** pondrás / vayas
- **C** pondrás / irás
- **B** pongas / vayas
- **D** pongas / irás

5. Cuando ... la verdad, no lo ...

- **A** conocerán / creerán
- **C** conozcan / creerán
- **B** conocerán / crean
- **D** conozcan / crean

6. El día en que ... a España, ... quedarse.

- **A** irá / querrá
- **C** irá / quiera
- **B** vaya / quiera
- **D** vaya / querrá

Select the correct translation for each sentence.

Answers page 259

1. I don't know what time I will go out.

- **A** No sé a qué hora salga.
- **B** No sé a qué hora saldré.

2. Do as you wish.

- **A** Haced lo que queráis.
- **B** Haced lo que querréis.

3. Tell me how you will do it.

- **A** Dime cómo lo hagas.
- **B** Dime cómo lo harás.

4. I am sure that he will not tell you.

- **A** Estoy seguro de que no te lo diga.
- **B** Estoy seguro de que no te lo dirá.

5. I don't know when it will be possible.

- **A** No sé cuándo sea posible.
- **B** No sé cuándo será posible.

6. When it will be possible, I will tell you.

- **A** Cuando sea posible te lo diré.
- **B** Cuando será posible te lo diré.

7. I will do what you say.

- **A** Haré lo que digas.
- **B** Haré lo que dirás.

8. Go out with who you fancy.

- **A** Sal con quien te apetezca.
- **B** Sal con quien te apetece.

Verbs

almacenar	*to store, to stock, to archive*
cargar	*to load, to charge*
colgar	*to hang, to upload, to post online* (**quedarse colgado** *to crash, to freeze,* i.e. a computer) (verb with a spelling change)
descansar	*to rest*
descargar	*to unload, to download*
enchufar	*to plug in*
medir	*to measure* (verb with a spelling change)
navegar	*to navigate, to browse* (the Internet)
pesar	*to weigh*
pinchar	*to click* (another alternative is **hacer clic**)

IT vocabulary

el archivo	*file, archive*
la batería	*battery*
la búsqueda	*search*
el cargador	*charger*
la carpeta	*folder*
la contraseña	*password*
el dato	*data*
el disco	*disc*
el dispositivo	*device*
el enlace	*link*
el escritorio	*desk, desktop*
el fichero	*file*

Unit 26
ÚTILES

inalámbrico/a	*wireless, cordless* (m./f.)
el lápiz	*pencil, USB drive*
el ordenador	*computer* (**el ordenador de escritorio** or **de sobremesa** *desktop computer, PC*)
la pantalla	*screen*
el pen	*USB drive*
el pincho	*USB drive*
el portátil	*laptop* (computer)
el ratón	*mouse*
la tecla	*key, button*
el teclado	*keyboard, keypad*
el vínculo	*link*
el virus	*virus*

Talking about 'when'

a cada rato	*often, frequently*
el jueves próximo	*next Thursday*
la semana que viene	*next week*
mañana	*tomorrow*
pasado mañana	*the day after tomorrow, for the next two days*
pronto	*soon*

ESENCIALES

PAGE 250
Size and weight
1 **C** 2 **B** 3 **A** 4 **A**

Fractions, decimals, percentages and proportions
1 **C** 2 **A** 3 **C** 4 **A** 5 **B** 6 **A**, **B** 7 **A** 8 **A**, **C**

PAGE 251
IT vocabulary
1 **B** 2 **A** 3 **B** 4 **C** 5 **A**, **B**, **C** 6 **B**
1 **A**, **B** 2 **A**, **B** 3 **B** 4 **A**, **B** 5 **B**, **C** 6 **A**
1 **E** 2 **A** 3 **C** 4 **D** 5 **F** 6 **A**, **B**, **C**

PAGE 253
Relative pronouns
1 **A**, **B** 2 **A**, **B** 3 **B** 4 **A**, **B** 5 **B** 6 **A**, **B** 7 **B** 8 **B** 9 **B** 8 **A**, **B**

PAGE 254
Any, whichever, anyone, any old, etc.
1 **B** 2 **A** 3 **A** 4 **A** 5 **B** 6 **B** 7 **A** 8 **B**

PAGE 255
Talking about the future
1 **B** 2 **A** 3 **C** 4 **A** 5 **B** 6 **B**

Tense sequence in the future
1 **D** 2 **B** 3 **C** 4 **A** 5 **C** 6 **D**
1 **B** 2 **A** 3 **B** 4 **B** 5 **B** 6 **A** 7 **A** 8 **A**

YOUR
SCORE:

Did you get between 0 and 12? ¡Ay, ay, ay!

Did you get between 13 and 26? Muy justito...

Did you get between 27 and 40? No está mal, pero...

Did you get between 41 and 54? Enhorabuena.

Did you get 55 or over? ¡Eres un auténtico fenómeno!

Tema **Travelling**

Answers page 270

Select the Spanish equivalent in each case.

1. Aisle or window?

   A ¿Pasillo o ventanilla?
   B ¿Pasilla o ventanillo?
   C ¿Corredor o ventana?

2. a low-cost ticket

   A un boleto a bajo costo
   B un billete de bajo coste
   C un tique de baja costa

3. train station

   A la estación
   B la garra
   C el estacionamiento

4. carpooling / ridesharing

   A la cococha
   B el cococche
   C el coche compartido

5. round trip / return trip

   A ida y vuelta
   B ido y vuelto
   C ido y venido

6. train platform

   A qué
   B embarque
   C andén

7. price / fare

   A el tarifo
   B la tarifa
   C el tarife

8. departure

   A el puerto
   B la salida
   C el deporte

Tema **Flying**

Choose the most appropriate term to complete each sentence. More than one answer may be possible.

Answers page 27

1. Voy a facturar ...

   A tripulación.
   B equipaje.
   C maletas.

2. Bienvenidos a bordo, les saludan el comandante y ...

   A el equipaje.
   B la tripulación.
   C las azafatas.

3. Abróchense ...

   A la cintura de seguro.

   B el cinturón de seguridad.

   C la cinta del seguro.

4. Apaguen los móviles durante ...

   A el despegue.

   B el descuelle.

   C el embarque.

5. Permanezcan en sus ... durante el aterrizaje.

   A sillas

   B sillones

   C asientos

6. Presenten el DNI y ...

   A el mapa de embarcar.

   B la carta de embarco.

   C la tarjeta de embarque.

7. El vuelo tiene ...

   A retraso.

   B retardo.

   C trasero.

8. ... el avión.

   A He fracasado

   B He perdido

   C He roto

Tema **Some common expressions based on animals**

Choose the Spanish expression that conveys the same meaning.

Answers page 270

1. to go crazy, to go wild

   A estar como un burro

   C estar como una cabra

   B estar como una rana

2. to be bored to death

   A aburrirse como una tortuga

   C aburrirse como un caracol

   B aburrirse como una ostra

3. to be bad-tempered

   A tener malas pulgas

   C tener malos mosquitos

   B tener malas moscas

4. There must be a catch.

   A Hay loro encerrado.

   C Hay gato encerrado.

   B Hay caballo encerrado.

5. to take the rap, to take the blame

Ⓐ pagar el pato   Ⓒ pagar el toro

Ⓑ pagar la vaca

6. to sleep it off

Ⓐ dormir la mona   Ⓒ dormir la oveja

Ⓑ dormir el zorro

7. to hit two birds with one stone

Ⓐ matar dos elefantes de un tiro   Ⓒ matar dos leones de un tiro

Ⓑ matar dos pájaros de un tiro

8. the awkward age

Ⓐ la edad del oso   Ⓒ la edad del pavo

Ⓑ la edad de la mariposa

Tema *Por* or *para*?

Choose the correct preposition for each context.

Answers
page 270

1. Me gusta viajar ... la noche.

Ⓐ para   Ⓑ por

2. Quisiera un billete ... la semana que viene.

Ⓐ para   Ⓑ por

3. Quisiéramos dos billetes ... Madrid.

Ⓐ para   Ⓑ por

4. ... aprender idiomas, lo mejor es viajar.

Ⓐ Para   Ⓑ Por

5. Voy a vivir a Cádiz ... un año.

Ⓐ para   Ⓑ por

6. Los viajes son buenos ... la salud.

Ⓐ para   Ⓑ por

7. No tengo mucho dinero, ... eso viajo poco.

    Ⓐ para   Ⓑ por

8. Me gusta mirar ... la ventanilla del tren.

    Ⓐ para   Ⓑ por

9. ¿Hay descuentos ... jubilados?

    Ⓐ para   Ⓑ por

10. ... usted, ¿cuál es la ciudad española más agradable?

    Ⓐ Para   Ⓑ Por

11. Tengo un regalo ... ti.

    Ⓐ para   Ⓑ por

12. ... ir a Madrid, ¿... dónde pasas?

    Ⓐ Para / para   Ⓑ Por / para

    Ⓒ Para / por   Ⓓ Por / por

Tema **Relative pronouns**

*Select the correct option to complete each sentence. More than one answer may
be possible.*

**Answers
page 270**

1. La persona con ... viajo.

    Ⓐ la que   Ⓑ quien   Ⓒ que

2. Tengo unos primos ... siempre me invitan a España.

    Ⓐ quien   Ⓑ a quienes   Ⓒ que

3. Hay gente ... no me gusta como compañera de viaje.

    Ⓐ la que   Ⓑ quienes   Ⓒ que

4. Hay personas ... no se me ocurre invitar.

    Ⓐ que   Ⓑ a quienes   Ⓒ a las que

5. Viajar sin prisa: eso es ... que hay que hacer.

    Ⓐ que   Ⓑ lo que   Ⓒ la que

6. ¿Conoces a aquel hombre ... lleva una maleta?

   A al que
   B que
   C quien

7. ¿Es suyo el perro ... está corriendo por el pasillo?

   A quien
   B que
   C el que

8. He conocido a esas chicas ... siempre me hablas.

   A que
   B de las que
   C de quienes

Choose the sentence the relative pronoun belongs in.

1. con el que

   A Este es el viaje ... sueño.

   B Esta es la maleta ... viajo.

   C Este es el medio de transporte ... prefiero.

   Answers page 270

2. en quien

   A El coche ... estás pensando es demasiado caro.

   B El trayecto ... estás pensando no es el mejor.

   C La chica ... estás pensando no te conviene.

3. a la que

   A Es la última vez ... te lo digo.

   B Es la última persona ... quiero ver.

   C Es la última cosa ... me apetece comer.

4. de quienes

   A Hay cosas ... no me acuerdo.

   B Hay amigos ... no me acuerdo nunca.

   C Hay amigas ... no recuerdo.

5. por las que

   A Hay calles ... no se me ocurre pasar.

   B Hay países ... no tengo ganas de visitar.

   C Hay ropa ... no me gusta llevar.

6. para los que

  Ⓐ Hay ideas ... no soy partidario.

  Ⓑ Tienes problemas ... no existe solución.

  Ⓒ Hay sitios ... no viajaré nunca.

Tema **Expressing 'hopefully'**

*Based on the elements provided, choose the correct construction with **ojalá**.*

1. vosotros / perder el tren

  Ⓐ Ojalá no pierdáis el tren.

  Ⓑ Ojalá no perdéis el tren.

  Ⓒ Ojalá no perdáis el tren.

Answers page 270

2. yo / jubilarse

  Ⓐ Ojalá me jubile pronto.

  Ⓑ Ojalá me jubila pronto.

  Ⓒ Ojalá me jubilo pronto.

3. nosotros / dar la vuelta al mundo

  Ⓐ Ojalá demos la vuelta al mundo un día.

  Ⓑ Ojalá doyemos la vuelta al mundo un día.

  Ⓒ Ojalá daramos la vuelta al mundo un día.

4. los billetes / costar caro

  Ⓐ Ojalá no costen caro los billetes.

  Ⓑ Ojalá no cuestan caro los billetes.

  Ⓒ Ojalá no cuesten caro los billetes.

5. tú / saber la verdad

  Ⓐ Ojalá no sabas nunca la verdad.

  Ⓑ Ojalá no sepas nunca la verdad.

  Ⓒ Ojalá no seas nunca la verdad.

6. hacer buen tiempo

Ⓐ Ojalá haya buen tiempo.

Ⓑ Ojalá haga buen tiempo.

Ⓒ Ojalá haiga buen tiempo.

| **Tema** | **Asking politely in the conditional** |

Select the equivalent question in the conditional.

Answers
page 270

1. ¿Por cuánto sale el viaje?

Ⓐ ¿Por cuánto saldrá el viaje?   Ⓒ ¿Por cuánto saldría el viaje?

Ⓑ ¿Por cuánto salía el viaje?

2. ¿Vais con él al cine?

Ⓐ ¿Iríais con él al cine?   Ⓒ ¿Ibais con él al cine?

Ⓑ ¿Irías con él al cine?

3. ¿Ves algún problema?

Ⓐ ¿Verías algún problema?   Ⓒ ¿Veríais algún problema?

Ⓑ ¿Verás algún problema?

4. ¿Hay billetes?

Ⓐ ¿Habría billetes?   Ⓒ ¿Haría billetes?

Ⓑ ¿Haya billetes?

5. ¿Me hacéis un favor?

Ⓐ ¿Me hacíais un favor?   Ⓒ ¿Me haríais un favor?

Ⓑ ¿Me habríais un favor?

6. ¿Me pides una cerveza?

Ⓐ ¿Me pedirás una cerveza?   Ⓒ ¿Me pidirías una cerveza?

Ⓑ ¿Me pedirías una cerveza?

| Tema | Tense sequence |

For each context, select the correct verb form in the subordinate clause.

Answers
page 270

1. En cuanto ..., iba a España.

   Ⓐ podía   Ⓑ pude   Ⓒ pueda   Ⓓ puedo

2. En cuanto ..., viviré en España.

   Ⓐ podía   Ⓑ pude   Ⓒ pueda   Ⓓ puedo

3. En cuanto ..., compré un billete para España.

   Ⓐ podía   Ⓑ pude   Ⓒ pueda   Ⓓ puedo

4. En cuanto ..., viajo a España.

   Ⓐ podía   Ⓑ pude   Ⓒ pueda   Ⓓ puedo

Select the correct main clause for each subordinate clause provided. More than one option may be possible.

Answers
page 270

1. Mientras no tienes la tarjeta de embarque,

   Ⓐ ... no estarás tranquilo.   Ⓒ ... no estuviste tranquilo.

   Ⓑ ... no estás tranquilo.   Ⓓ ... no estabas tranquilo.

2. Mientras viajabas...,

   Ⓐ ... yo me quedaría en casa.   Ⓒ ... yo me quedaré en casa.

   Ⓑ ... yo me quedaba en casa.   Ⓓ ... yo me quedo en casa.

3. Mientras estuvisteis de viaje,

   Ⓐ ... no nos movimos de aquí.   Ⓒ ... no nos moveremos de aquí.

   Ⓑ ... no nos movemos de aquí.   Ⓓ ... no nos moveríamos de aquí.

4. Mientras seáis jóvenes,

   Ⓐ ... viajad.   Ⓒ ... viajaréis.

   Ⓑ ... viajabais.   Ⓓ ... viajasteis.

5. Mientras tengáis dinero,

   Ⓐ ... disfrutasteis de la vida.   Ⓒ ... disfrutais de la vida.

   Ⓑ ... disfrutabais de la vida.   Ⓓ ... disfrutaréis de la vida.

Unit 27
ÚTILES

Verbs

abrochar	*to button, to fasten*
aburrirse	*to be bored*
apagar	*to switch off, to turn off*
correr	*to run*
disfrutar	*to enjoy*
encerrar	*to enclose, to shut away* (verb with a spelling change)
facturar	*to check in, to check baggage*
fracasar	*to fail, to be unsuccessful*
jubilarse	*to retire*
matar	*to kill*
perder	*to miss (a train or plane)* (verb with a spelling change)
permanecer	*to remain, to stay*
viajar	*to travel*

More verbs

dar la vuelta al mundo	*to go around the world*
salir por	*to cost (a certain price)*
soñar con	*to dream of* (verb with a spelling change)

Animals

el burro	*donkey*
el caballo	*horse*
la cabra	*goat*
el caracol	*snail*
el elefante	*elephant*
el gato	*cat*
el león	*lion*

el loro	parrot
la mariposa	butterfly
el mono	monkey
la mosca	fly
el mosquito	mosquito
el oso	bear
la oveja	sheep
el pájaro	bird
el pavo	turkey
la pulga	flea
la rana	frog
la tortuga	tortoise, turtle
el zorro	fox

Travel and transport vocabulary

el asiento	seat
el azafato / la azafata	flight attendant (m./f.)
el cinturón de seguridad	seat belt
el despegue	take-off
el embarque	boarding
el equipaje	luggage, baggage
la tarjeta de embarque	boarding pass
la maleta	suitcase, bag
el retraso	delay
el trayecto	route, journey
la tripulación	crew
el viaje	trip, voyage

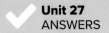

Unit 27
ANSWERS

ESENCIALES

PAGE 260
Travelling
1 **A** 2 **B** 3 **A** 4 **C** 5 **A** 6 **C** 7 **B** 8 **B**

Flying
1 **B, C** 2 **B, C** 3 **B** 4 **A** 5 **C** 6 **C** 7 **A** 8 **B**

PAGE 261
Some common expressions based on animals
1 **C** 2 **B** 3 **A** 4 **C** 5 **A** 6 **A** 7 **B** 8 **C**

PAGE 262
Por or *para*?
1 **B** 2 **A** 3 **A** 4 **A** 5 **B** 6 **A** 7 **B** 8 **B** 9 **A** 10 **A** 11 **A** 12 **C**

PAGE 263
Relative pronouns
1 **A, B** 2 **C** 3 **C** 4 **A, B, C** 5 **B** 6 **B** 7 **B** 8 **B, C**
1 **A** 2 **C** 3 **B** 4 **B** 5 **A** 6 **B**

PAGE 265
Expressing 'hopefully'
1 **C** 2 **A** 3 **A** 4 **C** 5 **B** 6 **B**

PAGE 266
Asking politely in the conditional
1 **C** 2 **A** 3 **A** 4 **A** 5 **C** 6 **B**

PAGE 267
Tense sequence
1 **A** 2 **C** 3 **B** 4 **D**
1 **B** 2 **B** 3 **A** 4 **A C** 5 **D**

YOUR
SCORE:

Did you get between 0 and 14? ¡Ay, ay, ay!

Did you get between 15 and 28? Muy justito...

Did you get between 29 and 42? No está mal, pero...

Did you get between 43 and 56? Enhorabuena.

Did you get 57 or over? ¡Eres un auténtico fenómeno!

Tema Asking for help at the hotel

Select the correct ending for the incomplete word in each sentence.

Answers
page 279

1. El col... es demasiado blando.

   A ... da   B ... chón   C ... fo

   D ... jo   E ... nado

2. La almoha ... no tiene funda.

   A ... da   B ... chón   C ... fo

   D ... jo   E ... nado

3. El aire acondicio... no funciona.

   A ... da   B ... chón   C ... fo

   D ... jo   E ... nado

4. El gri... gotea.

   A ... da   B ... chón   C ... fo

   D ... jo   E ... nado

5. El espe... está roto.

   A ... da   B ... chón   C ... fo

   D ... jo   E ... nado

Now select the correct beginning for the incomplete word.

Answers
page 279

1. Las ...tas están agujereadas.

   A sá...   B man...   C fun...

   D bom...   E cale...

2. Las ...billas están fundidas.

   A sá...   B man...   C fun...

   D bom...   E cale...

3. La ...facción está averiada.

   A sá...   B man...   C fun...

   D bom...   E cale...

4. Las ...banas están gastadas.

A. sá...   B. man...   C. fun...

D. bom...   E. cale...

5. Las ...das están sucias.

A. sá...   B. man...   C. fun...

D. bom...   E. cale...

Tema | Giving an opinion

Choose the correct way to introduce each sentence.

Answers page 279

1. ..., este hotel es malísimo.

A. A mi opinión   B. Por mi opinión   C. En mi opinión

2. ..., el precio es demasiado alto.

A. Según yo   B. Según me   C. Según mí

3. ... las valoraciones son bastante negativas.

A. Tengo la sensación que   B. Tengo la sensación de que   C. Tengo la sensación en que

4. ... que hay poca clientela.

A. Me parece   B. Parezco   C. Me parezco

5. ..., deberían cambiar la decoración.

A. En mi juicio   B. Por mi juicio   C. A mi juicio

6. ..., las habitaciones son incómodas.

A. A mi punto de vista   B. En mi punto de vista   C. Desde mi punto de vista

Tema | Saying 'when'

Choose the equivalent translation in each case.

Answers page 279

1. I would like a room for next Thursday.

A. Quisiera una habitación para el jueves próximo.

B. Quisiera una habitación para los jueves próximos.

2. Is the reception desk open on Saturdays?

   Ⓐ ¿Está abierta la recepción los sábados?

   Ⓑ ¿Está abierta la recepción el sábado?

3. On Tuesdays I go to the swimming pool.

   Ⓐ El martes voy a la piscina.

   Ⓑ Los martes voy a la piscina.

4. Today is Tuesday the 4th.

   Ⓐ Hoy es martes 4.

   Ⓑ Hoy es los martes 4.

5. I will be out of the room on Monday.

   Ⓐ Dejaré la habitación el lunes.

   Ⓑ Dejaré la habitación los lunes.

6. I will arrive on Wednesday.

   Ⓐ Llegaré el miércoles.

   Ⓑ Llegaré los miércoles.

Tema   **Expressing doubt**

Answers page 279

Choose the option that expresses the same doubt in a different way.

1. Tal vez haya habitaciones con vistas al mar, pero las nuestras no las tienen.

   Ⓐ Hará habitaciones con vistas al mar, pero las nuestras no las tienen.

   Ⓑ Habrá habitaciones con vistas al mar, pero las nuestras no las tienen.

2. A lo mejor sale un poco caro, pero merece la pena.

   Ⓐ Saldré un poco caro, pero merece la pena.

   Ⓑ Saldrá un poco caro, pero merece la pena.

3. Quizás muchos se quejen sin razón, pero no me fío de ese hotel.

   Ⓐ Muchos se quejarán sin razón, pero no me fío de ese hotel.

   Ⓑ Muchos se querrán sin razón, pero no me fío de ese hotel.

4. Puede que vosotros le veáis ventajas, pero a mí no me convence.

   (A) Vosotros le vayáis ventajas, pero a mí no me convence.

   (B) Vosotros le veréis ventajas, pero a mí no me convence.

5. Tal vez no haya hecho nada malo, pero todos lo critican.

   (A) No habrá hecho nada malo, pero todos lo critican.

   (B) No hará hecho nada malo, pero todos lo critican.

6. A lo mejor dan buenos desayunos, pero los cuartos están sucios.

   (A) Dirán buenos desayunos, pero los cuartos están sucios.

   (B) Darán buenos desayunos, pero los cuartos están sucios.

Tema | **The passive voice**

Select the equivalent in the passive voice.

Answers page 279

1. Los clientes han valorado negativamente estos establecimientos.

   (A) Estos establecimientos han habidos valorados negativamente por los clientes.

   (B) Estos establecimientos han sido valorados negativamente por los clientes.

2. El hotel no acepta pagos en efectivo.

   (A) Los pagos en efectivo no han aceptados por el hotel.

   (B) Los pagos en efectivo no son aceptados por el hotel.

3. Los usuarios eligieron este hotel mejor establecimiento del año.

   (A) Este hotel fue elegido por los usuarios mejor establecimiento del año.

   (B) Este hotel estuvo elegido por los usuarios mejor establecimiento del año.

4. Cientos de usuarios verán estas valoraciones.

   (A) Estas valoraciones serán vistas por cientos de usuarios.

   (B) Estas valoraciones sean vidas por cientos de usuarios.

5. Clientes insatisfechos escribían la mayor parte de los comentarios.

   (A) La mayor parte de los comentarios eran escritos por clientes insatisfechos.

   (B) La mayor parte de los comentarios estaban escriptos por clientes insatisfechos.

In general, Spanish keeps things simple and uses the active rather than the passive voice. While the following passive sentences are grammatically correct, they aren't very natural in Spanish. Select the equivalent in the active voice.

1. No creo que los grifos sean rotos por los clientes.

    A No creo que los clientes rompan los grifos.

    B No creo que los clientes rompen los grifos.

2. Los clientes son satisfechos por el servicio.

    A El servicio satisface a los clientes.

    B El servicio satisfecha a los clientes.

3. Esta foto fue hecha por un cliente.

    A Un cliente hizo esta foto.

    B Un cliente hice esta foto.

4. En caso de robo, una denuncia sería puesta por las víctimas.

    A En caso de robo, las víctimas podrían una denuncia.

    B En caso de robo, las víctimas pondrían una denuncia.

5. Si hay un problema, el dinero le será devuelto por el hotel.

    A Si hay un problema, el hotel le devolverá el dinero.

    B Si hay un problema, el hotel le devuelverá el dinero.

| **Tema** | **Describing when something happened** |

Select the verb tense that corresponds to the rest of the sentence.

Answers page 279

1. La piscina ... abierta pasado mañana.

    A estuvo   B estará

2. ¿... ustedes una habitación para la semana que viene?

    A Tendrían   B Tuvieron

3. Anteayer ... habitaciones exteriores, pero ya no hay.

    A había   B habrá

4. Anoche ... demasiado calor en la habitación.

    A tendremos   B tuvimos

Unit 28
ESENCIALES

5. ... saber si tienen habitaciones con cama supletoria para mañana.

   Ⓐ Quise   Ⓑ Quisiera

Now select the time term that corresponds to the meaning of the sentence.

Answers page 279

1. ... hizo mucho frío en nuestro cuarto.

   Ⓐ Anteanoche   Ⓑ El lunes próximo

2. ... nos dijeron que la primera planta era muy ruidosa.

   Ⓐ Dentro de una hora   Ⓑ Ayer

3. ... nos quejaremos del servicio.

   Ⓐ Mañana   Ⓑ La semana pasada

4. ... reservaré en otro hotel.

   Ⓐ La última vez   Ⓑ La próxima vez

5. ... un cliente se ahogó en la piscina.

   Ⓐ Dentro de poco   Ⓑ Hace un tiempo

Tema   **Conjugating the verb *oler* (to smell)**

*Select the correct conjugated form of **oler** to complete each sentence.*   **Answers page 279**

1. Yo no ... nada, ¿y tú? (present tense)

   Ⓐ olo   Ⓑ uelo   Ⓒ huelo   Ⓓ uhelo

2. ¿No ... a quemado? (present tense)

   Ⓐ oléis   Ⓑ holéis   Ⓒ ueléis   Ⓓ ueléis

3. En aquel hotel ... a basura. (imperfect tense)

   Ⓐ olía   Ⓑ olaba   Ⓒ holía   Ⓓ huelía

4. Con la barbacoa, las manos me ... a sardina todo el día. (preterite tense)

   Ⓐ holieron   Ⓑ olieron   Ⓒ uelieron   Ⓓ huelieron

5. Si no os ducháis después del deporte, ... mal. (future tense)

   Ⓐ oleréis   Ⓑ holeréis   Ⓒ hueleréis   Ⓓ ueleréis

6. Con un poco de colonia, ... mejor. (conditional)

   A holeríamos   B ueleríamos   C hueleríamos   D oleríamos

7. Quiero que ... este queso. (present subjunctive)

   A olas   B huelas   C holas   D uelas

Verbs

ÚTILES

ahogarse	*to drown*
cerrar	*to close* (verb with a spelling change)
criticar	*to criticize*
fiarse	*to trust*
funcionar	*to function, to work*
gotear	*to drip, to leak*
merecer	*to deserve, to merit*
oler	*to smell* (irregular in the present indicative & subjunctive, e.g. **huelo** / *smell*)
quejarse	*to complain*
satisfacer	*to satisfy*
valorar	*to value, to assess*

Hotel vocabulary

el aire acondicionado	*air-conditioning*
la almohada	*pillow*
la basura	*rubbish, garbage, trash*
la bombilla	*lightbulb*
la calefacción	*heating*
la cama supletoria	*extra bed*
el colchón	*mattress*
la decoración	*decoration, décor*

Unit 28
ÚTILES

el espejo	*mirror*
exterior	*facing out* (a room facing the street)
la funda	*pillowcase*
el grifo	*tap, faucet*
la habitación	*room*
interior	*facing in* (a room not overlooking the street)
la manta	*blanket*
la planta	*floor, level*
la sábana	*sheet* (bed)
con vistas a	*with a view of, overlooking*

Reporting problems

agujereado/a	*full of holes* (m./f.)
averiado/a	*broken, out of order* (m./f.)
blando/a	*soft* (m./f.)
el calor	*heat* (**Hace calor.** *It's hot.*)
fundido/a	*blown, burned out* (e.g. a lightbulb) (m./f.)
gastado/a	*worn out, threadbare* (m./f.)
incómodo/a	*uncomfortable* (m./f.)
frío/a	*cold* (**Hace frío.** *It's cold.*)
sucio/a	*dirty, filthy* (m./f.)
usuario/a	*user* (m./f.)
la ventaja	*advantage, benefit*

ESENCIALES

PAGE 271
Asking for help at the hotel
1 B 2 A 3 E 4 C 5 D
1 B 2 D 3 E 4 A 5 C

PAGE 272
Giving an opinion
1 C 2 A 3 B 4 A 5 C 6 C

Saying 'when'
1 A 2 A 3 B 4 A 5 A 6 A

PAGE 273
Expressing doubt
1 B 2 B 3 A 4 B 5 A 6 B

PAGE 274
The passive voice
1 B 2 B 3 A 4 A 5 A
1 A 2 A 3 A 4 B 5 A

PAGE 275
Describing when something happened
1 B 2 A 3 A 4 B 5 B
1 A 2 B 3 A 4 B 5 B

PAGE 276
Conjugating the verb *oler* (to smell)
1 C 2 A 3 A 4 B 5 A 6 D 7 B

YOUR
SCORE:

Did you get between 0 and 10? ¡Ay, ay, ay!

Did you get between 11 and 21? Muy justito...

Did you get between 22 and 32? No está mal, pero...

Did you get between 33 and 43? Enhorabuena.

Did you get 44 or over? ¡Eres un auténtico fenómeno!

Tema	**Creating nouns from adjectives**

Select the correct noun that corresponds to each adjective.

Answers
page 289

1. tonto
   - A tontedad
   - B tontería
   - C tonteza

2. solo
   - A solitud
   - B soledad
   - C solera

3. alegre
   - A alegreza
   - B alegridad
   - C alegría

4. aburrido
   - A aburrición
   - B aburrimiento
   - C aburridad

5. viejo
   - A viejera
   - B viejedad
   - C vejez

6. joven
   - A jovineza
   - B juventud
   - C jovenez

7. lento
   - A lentitud
   - B lentera
   - C lentedad

8. rápido
   - A rapidez
   - B rapidad
   - C rapididad

9. enfermo
   - A enfermitud
   - B enfermidad
   - C enfermedad

10. bueno
    - A buendad
    - B bondad
    - C buenitud

11. sucio
    - A sucieza
    - B suciera
    - C suciedad

12. nervioso
    - A nerviosidad
    - B nerviosismo
    - C nervositud

| **Tema** | **Scene, stage or screenplay?** |

Choose the most appropriate word for each context.

Answers
page 289

1. Los actores se suben ...

    A a la escena.   B al escenario.   C al guion.

2. Si compramos entradas de primera fila, estaremos más cerca ...

    A de la escena.   B del escenario.   C del guion.

3. Me ha gustado ... de esta película, pero los actores eran muy malos.

    A la escena   B el escenario   C el guion

4. ... final de la obra me ha encantado.

    A La escena   B El escenario   C El guion

5. La serie no está mal, pero sobran ...

    A algunas escenas.   B algunos escenarios.   C algunos guiones.

6. ... de la peli no es muy original: están la mujer, el marido y el amante.

    A La escena   B El escenario   C El guion

7. La puesta en ... de la obra era divertida.

    A escena   B escenario   C guion

8. Es una obra de teatro espectacular: hay decenas de actores en ...

    A la escena.   B el escenario.   C el guion.

| **Tema** | **Going to a performance** |

Choose the appropriate option to complete each sentence. More than one answer may be possible.

Answers
page 289

1. Quisiera dos ... para la ópera Carmen.

    A tiques   B entradas   C plazas

2. Quedan localidades en ...

    A el patio de butacas.   B los sillones de orquesta.   C las sillas de plata.

3. La primera representación de una obra de teatro se llama ...

   A la prima.   B el estreno.   C la entrada.

4. Me han invitado a asistir a ... de la obra.

   A las repeticiones   B las pruebas   C los ensayos

5. Pedro Almodóvar es a la vez ... y ...

   A realizador /   B director /   C director /
     escenarista.   guionista.   escenarista.

6. El actor es guapo, pero su ... es malísima.

   A actuación   B juego   C interpretación

7. ¿Compramos ... de maíz para la peli?

   A palomitos   B palomitas   C palomas

8. ¡Esta película es malísima, un verdadero ...!

   A nabo   B puerro   C rollo

Tema **Expressing physical sensations**

Select the most likely physical sensation in each context to complete these sentences.

1. Soy vegano. Cuando veo a gente que come carne, me da ...

   A asco.   B calor.   C frío.

   D hambre.   E sed.   F sueño.

Answers page 289

2. Cuando la película es mala y larga, me da ...

   A asco.   B calor.   C frío.

   D hambre.   E sed.   F sueño.

3. Cuando veo una bolsa de patatas fritas, me da ...

   A asco.   B calor.   C frío.

   D hambre.   E sed.   F sueño.

4. En verano, cuando veo una cerveza fresquita, me da ...

   A asco.   B calor.   C frío.

   D hambre.   E sed.   F sueño.

5. Este jersey es demasiado gordo. Me da ...

   A asco.   B calor.   C frío.

   D hambre.   E sed.   F sueño.

6. Cuando te veo con camisa de manga corta en invierno, me da ...

   A asco.   B calor.   C frío.

   D hambre.   E sed.   F sueño.

Tema Expressing feelings

Choose the most probable feeling in each context.

1. Estoy furiosa contigo, me da ... tu egoísmo.

   A gusto   B lástima   C miedo

   D pereza   E rabia   F vergüenza

Answers page 289

2. Soy muy tímido, me da ... hablar en público.

   A gusto   B lástima   C miedo

   D pereza   E rabia   F vergüenza

3. Estoy contento de verte. Me da ... saludarte.

   A gusto   B lástima   C miedo

   D pereza   E rabia   F vergüenza

4. Estoy muy cansado. Me da ... salir ahora.

   A gusto   B lástima   C miedo

   D pereza   E rabia   F vergüenza

5. Me gustan los animales y me da ... verlos encerrados en un zoológico.

   A gusto   B lástima   C miedo

   D pereza   E rabia   F vergüenza

6. Me da ... el cine de terror.

   A gusto   B lástima   C miedo

   D pereza   E rabia   F vergüenza

Unit 29
ESENCIALES

Answers
page 289

Tema Using *dar* + noun to express a feeling

Select the correct translation in each case.

1. It disgusted me to see him eat with his fingers.

   Ⓐ Me dio asco verlo comer con los dedos.

   Ⓑ Me dó asco de verlo comer con los dedos.

2. I'm ashamed of you.

   Ⓐ Os doy vergüenza.

   Ⓑ Me dais vergüenza.

3. Films that are too long make them sleepy.

   Ⓐ Las películas demasiado largas les dabían sueño.

   Ⓑ Las películas demasiado largas les daban sueño.

4. We would regret not seeing that exhibition.

   Ⓐ Nos daría lástima no ver esa exposición.

   Ⓑ Nos daríamos lástima no ver esa exposición.

5. Ice creams make them feel cold.

   Ⓐ Le dan frío los helados.

   Ⓑ Les dan frío los helados.

6. I don't believe that these stories make you scared.

   Ⓐ No creo que te den miedo estas historias.

   Ⓑ No creo que te des miedo estas historias.

Tema Tense sequence

Select the correct equivalent expressed in the past.

Answers
page 289

1. Sabes que no me gusta el teatro, ¿verdad?

   Ⓐ Sabías que no me gustaba el teatro, ¿verdad?

   Ⓑ Sabías que no me gustaría el teatro, ¿verdad?

2. Estoy segura de que esta peli es un rollo.

   Ⓐ Estaba segura de que esta peli será un rollo.

   Ⓑ Estaba segura de que esta peli era un rollo.

3. Piensa que su obra emocionará al público.

   Ⓐ Pensó que su obra emocionaba al público.

   Ⓑ Pensó que su obra emocionaría al público.

4. Creo que habrá entradas para el estreno.

   Ⓐ Creía que habría entradas para el estreno.

   Ⓑ Creía que haya entradas para el estreno.

5. Sé lo que me vas a decir.

   Ⓐ Sabía lo que me vayas a decir.

   Ⓑ Sabía lo que me ibas a decir.

6. Estamos convencidos de que vendréis.

   Ⓐ Estábamos convencidos de que veníais.

   Ⓑ Estábamos convencidos de que vendríais.

Choose the correct form of the verb in each case. More than one may be possible.

1. Quería que ... conmigo al concierto.

   Ⓐ vengan   Ⓑ vinieran   Ⓒ viniesen

   Answers page 289

2. Le pedí al vecino que ...

   Ⓐ se callara.   Ⓑ se callará.   Ⓒ se callaría.

3. Se calló él solo. No hizo falta que se lo ...

   Ⓐ pediésemos.   Ⓑ pidiésemos.   Ⓒ pidáramos.

4. Me gustaría que ... más por el teatro de vanguardia.

   Ⓐ os interesarais   Ⓑ os interesaríais   Ⓒ os interesaréis

5. No vine para que me ... el coco con tus rollos.

   Ⓐ comerás　　　Ⓑ comieras　　　Ⓒ comieses

6. Mi novia tenía ganas de que yo ... a sus padres.

   Ⓐ conozciera　　　Ⓑ conozcara　　　Ⓒ conociera

Express these sentences in the past by selecting the correct ending.

1. Le digo que lo llamaré cuando deje de comerme el coco. / Le dije que lo ...

   Ⓐ ... llamara cuando dejaría de comerme el coco.

   Ⓑ ... llamaría cuando dejara de comerme el coco.

Answe
page 2

2. Nos recomiendan que veamos esta peli el día que tengamos tiempo. / Nos recomendaron que...

   Ⓐ ... veríamos esta peli el día que tendríamos tiempo.

   Ⓑ ... viéramos esta peli el día que tuviéramos tiempo.

3. Te pido que vayas con él al cine aunque no te apetezca. / Te pedí que ...

   Ⓐ ... fueras con él al cine aunque no te apeteciera.

   Ⓑ ... irías con él al cine aunque no te apetecería.

4. Sé que me diréis que no antes de que empiece a hablar. / Sabía que me ...

   Ⓐ ... diríais que no antes de que empezara a hablar.

   Ⓑ ... dijerais que no antes de que empezaría a hablar.

5. Me promete que lo hará en cuanto pueda. / Me prometió que lo ...

   Ⓐ ... haría en cuanto pudiese.

   Ⓑ ... hiciera en cuanto podría.

6. Dicen que seguirán viajando mientras sean jóvenes. / Decían que ...

   Ⓐ ... seguirían viajando mientras fueran jóvenes.

   Ⓑ ... siguieran viajando mientras fuesen jóvenes.

Tema | **Expressing hypothetical situations**

Select the correct translation for each sentence.

Answers
page 289

1. If you wanted to, we could go to the cinema.

   Ⓐ Si quisieras, podríamos ir al cine.

   Ⓑ Si quisieses, podamos ir al cine.

2. If we went to the cinema, would you buy me popcorn?

   Ⓐ Si fuéramos al cine, ¿me comprarías palomitas?

   Ⓑ Si íbamos al cine, ¿me comprabas palomitas?

3. If I grew a beard, would you love me?

   Ⓐ Si me dejaría la barba, ¿me querrás?

   Ⓑ Si me dejara la barba, ¿me querrías?

4. If you could agree, we would save time.

   Ⓐ Si os pusierais de acuerdo, ganaríamos tiempo.

   Ⓑ Si os pusieseis de acuerdo, ganaremos tiempo.

5. If they told you the truth, you wouldn't believe them.

   Ⓐ Si os digan la verdad, no los creeréis.

   Ⓑ Si os dijeran la verdad, no los creeríais.

6. If you read the newspapers, sir, you would know.

   Ⓐ Si leería los periódicos, caballero, lo supiera.

   Ⓑ Si leyera los periódicos, caballero, lo sabría.

Verbs | ÚTILES 💬

asistir	*to assist, to attend*
comer el coco	*to drive up the wall, to harass* (**el coco** *coconut* can also be used as slang for 'head')
emocionar	*to move, to arouse feeling*
prometer	*to promise*
recomendar	*to recommend* (verb with a spelling change)

Unit 29
ÚTILES

Expressing feelings or sensations

dar asco	*to disgust, to make sick*
dar gusto	*to make happy, to give pleasure*
dar pereza	*to not be bothered* ('to give laziness')
dar rabia	*to enrage, to make angry*
dar sed	*to make thirsty*
dar vergüenza	*to embarrass, to make ashamed*

Entertainment vocabulary

el director / la directora	*director* (m./f.)
el ensayo	*rehearsal*
el escenario	*stage* (in a theatre)
el estreno	*premiere, first night, opening*
la entrada	*ticket*
la escena	*scene*
el espectáculo	*show, performance*
el guion	*script, screenplay*
el/la guionista	*scriptwriter*
la interpretación	*interpretation, performance*
la actuación	*acting, performance*
la fila	*row, line*
la peli	*film* (shortened form of **la película**)
la localidad	*seat, ticket* (for a performance)
la obra	*work* (artistic creation)
la ópera	*opera*
la palomita de maíz	*popcorn*
el rollo	*drag, bore* (e.g. a bad film), *spiel, yarn* (a tiresome lecture or dubious story)

ESENCIALES

PAGE 280
Creating nouns from adjectives
1 **B** 2 **B** 3 **C** 4 **B** 5 **C** 6 **B** 7 **A** 8 **A** 9 **C** 10 **B** 11 **C** 12 **B**

PAGE 281
Scene, stage or screenplay?
1 **B** 2 **B** 3 **C** 4 **A** 5 **A** 6 **C** 7 **A** 8 **B**

Going to a performance
1 **B** 2 **A** 3 **B** 4 **C** 5 **B** 6 **AC** 7 **B** 8 **C**

PAGE 282
Expressing physical sensations
1 **A** 2 **F** 3 **D** 4 **E** 5 **B** 6 **C**

PAGE 283
Expressing feelings
1 **E** 2 **F** 3 **A** 4 **D** 5 **B** 6 **C**

PAGE 284
Using *dar* + noun to express a feeling
1 **A** 2 **B** 3 **B** 4 **A** 5 **B** 6 **A**

Tense sequence
1 **A** 2 **B** 3 **B** 4 **A** 5 **B** 6 **B**
1 **BC** 2 **A** 3 **B** 4 **A** 5 **BC** 6 **C**
1 **B** 2 **B** 3 **A** 4 **A** 5 **A** 6 **A**

PAGE 287
Expressing hypothetical situations
1 **A** 2 **A** 3 **B** 4 **A** 5 **B** 6 **B**

YOUR SCORE:

Did you get between 0 and 14? ¡Ay, ay, ay!

Did you get between 15 and 28? Muy justito...

Did you get between 29 and 42? No está mal, pero...

Did you get between 43 and 56? Enhorabuena.

Did you get 57 or over? ¡Eres un auténtico fenómeno!

...rts and physical activities

...Spanish equivalent for each of these sports.

Answers page 300

1. basketball
   - (A) baloncesto
   - (B) cestobol
   - (C) cestabol

2. handball
   - (A) manobol
   - (B) balonmano
   - (C) manobola

3. baseball
   - (A) béisbol
   - (B) bolabase
   - (C) basabola

4. boxing
   - (A) bóxing
   - (B) boxa
   - (C) boxeo

5. volleyball
   - (A) voleabol
   - (B) voleibol
   - (C) voleobol

6. fencing
   - (A) esgrima
   - (B) escrima
   - (C) sgrima

7. swimming
   - (A) nadación
   - (B) natación
   - (C) nadamiento

8. football / soccer
   - (A) fútbol
   - (B) piebalón
   - (C) futebol

9. hiking
   - (A) randóning
   - (B) cámining
   - (C) senderismo

10. tennis
    - (A) tenis
    - (B) tennis
    - (C) tenís

Choose the appropriate verb to complete each sentence.

Answers page 300

1. ¿Vienes a ... un partido de bádminton?
   - (A) jugar
   - (B) nadar
   - (C) pescar
   - (D) saltar

2. Voy a ... la maratón de Nueva York.
   A bucear   B correr   C escalar   D esquiar

3. Este año voy a aprender a ... con escafandra y botellas.
   A bucear   B correr   C escalar   D esquiar

4. Prefiero ... en altura que en longitud.
   A jugar   B nadar   C pescar   D saltar

5. En invierno voy a ... a Sierra Nevada.
   A bucear   B correr   C nadar   D esquiar

6. Hay que ser muy buen alpinista para ... un ocho mil.
   A bucear   B correr   C escalar   D esquiar

7. Mi deporte favorito es ...: ¡puedes practicarlo sentado!
   A jugar   B nadar   C pescar   D saltar

8. Prefiero ... en una piscina que en el mar.
   A jugar   B nadar   C pescar   D saltar

Tema Geography and landscapes

Choose the correct cardinal point for each context.

Answers page 300

1. No sé quién soy, he perdido el ...
   A norte.   B sur.   C este.   D oeste.

2. El sol se pone al ...
   A norte.   B sur.   C este.   D oeste.

3. Nueva York está en la costa ... de Estados Unidos.
   A norte   B sur   C este   D oeste

4. Andalucía es la región más al ... de España.
   A norte   B sur   C este   D oeste

...ct ending for the incomplete nature word in each case.

. gusta pasear por el bos...

A ...ano. **B** ...ba. **C** ...bol. **D** ...la.

E ...o. **F** ...po. **G** ...que. **H** te.

Answers page 300

2. Me encanta dormir la siesta a la sombra de un ár...

A ...ano. **B** ...ba. **C** ...bol. **D** ...la.

E ...o. **F** ...po. **G** ...que. **H** ...te.

3. Prefiero pasar las vacaciones en el cam...

A ...ano. **B** ...ba. **C** ...bol. **D** ...la.

E ...o. **F** ...po. **G** ...que. **H** ...te.

4. ¡Mira cómo comen hier... las vacas!

A ...ano **B** ...ba **C** ...bol **D** ...la

E ...o **F** ...po **G** ...que **H** ...te

5. Estoy harto de la ciudad, ¡me voy a vivir a una is... desierta!

A ...ano **B** ...ba **C** ...bol **D** ...la

E ...o **F** ...po **G** ...que **H** ...te

6. Dicen que hay lobos en el mon...

A ...ano. **B** ...ba. **C** ...bol. **D** ...la.

E ...o. **F** ...po. **G** ...que. **H** ...te.

7. Si vas a Cádiz, podrás hacer surf en el Océ... Atlántico.

A ...ano **B** ...ba **C** ...bol **D** ...la

E ...o **F** ...po **G** ...que **H** ...te

8. Voy a pescar al rí..., ¿vienes?

A ...ano **B** ...ba **C** ...bol **D** ...la

E ...o **F** ...po **G** ...que **H** ...te

Now choose the beginning of each nature word.

1. Dicen que hay un monstruo en este ...go.
   - A are...
   - B cie...
   - C es...
   - D la...
   - E lu...
   - F o...
   - G ori...
   - H pla...

2. Detesto viajar en barco cuando hay ...las.
   - A are...
   - B cie...
   - C es...
   - D la...
   - E lu...
   - F o...
   - G ori...
   - H pla...

3. El mar es peligroso: quédate en la ...lla.
   - A are...
   - B cie...
   - C es...
   - D la...
   - E lu...
   - F o...
   - G ori...
   - H pla...

4. ¡Qué azul está el ...lo hoy!
   - A are...
   - B cie...
   - C es...
   - D la...
   - E lu...
   - F o...
   - G ori...
   - H pla...

5. ¿Hacemos un castillo de ...na?
   - A are...
   - B cie...
   - C es...
   - D la...
   - E lu...
   - F o...
   - G ori...
   - H pla...

6. ¡Cómo brilla la ...na!
   - A are...
   - B cie...
   - C es...
   - D la...
   - E lu...
   - F o...
   - G ori...
   - H pla...

7. Algunas noches de verano, se pueden contar las ...trellas.
   - A are...
   - B cie...
   - C es...
   - D la...
   - E lu...
   - F o...
   - G ori...
   - H pla...

8. ¿Vamos a la ...ya?
   - A are...
   - B cie...
   - C es...
   - D la...
   - E lu...
   - F o...
   - G ori...
   - H pla...

Answ...
page 3

weather

appropriate adjective for each weather forecast.

Answers
page 300

1. Habrá bastantes nubes. El cielo estará ...

   A nubado.   B nublado.

2. Se prevé un cielo totalmente azul. El cielo estará...

   A despejado.   B despejoso.

3. Habrá muchísimas nubes. El cielo estará ...

   A cubierto.   B cubrido.

4. Las temperaturas no serán ni calientes ni frías. Tendremos un tiempo ...

   A templante.   B templado.

5. Lloverá. Se anuncia un tiempo ...

   A lluvioso.   B enlluviado.

6. Habrá sol en todas partes. Tendremos un tiempo ...

   A ensoleado.   B soleado.

7. Se esperan temperaturas muy altas. Se espera un tiempo ...

   A calente.   B caluroso.

8. Soplarán fuertes vientos. El día será muy ...

   A ventoso.   B vientoso.

9. Nevará durante la noche en el norte. El norte del país amanecerá ...

   A nevado.   B ennevado.

10. Helará en todo el país. Persistirá un ambiente ...

    A heloso.   B helado.

Tema Whatever, wherever, whenever, whoever, however ...

Choose the correct option for each context.

Answers page 300

1. Digas ... digas, no me convencerás.
   - **A** como
   - **B** cuando
   - **C** donde
   - **D** lo que
   - **E** quien

2. Paséis por ... paséis, es un viaje largo.
   - **A** como
   - **B** cuando
   - **C** donde
   - **D** lo que
   - **E** quien

3. Vengas ... vengas, aunque sea tarde, te abriré la puerta.
   - **A** como
   - **B** cuando
   - **C** donde
   - **D** lo que
   - **E** quien

4. Salgas con ... salgas, si lo quieres, no me importa.
   - **A** como
   - **B** cuando
   - **C** donde
   - **D** lo que
   - **E** quien

5. Juegues ... juegues, bien o mal, te queremos en nuestro equipo.
   - **A** como
   - **B** cuando
   - **C** donde
   - **D** lo que
   - **E** quien

Tema *Hacer or echar?*

Select the correct verb to complete each sentence.

Answers page 300

1. Has ... bien en venir.
   - **A** echo
   - **B** hecho

2. Te ... de menos.
   - **A** echo
   - **B** hecho

3. He ... de menos España.
   - **A** echado
   - **B** hechado

…arta al buzón.

A Echo
B Hecho

5. ¿Qué pelis ...?

A echan
B hechan

6. Eso está ..., no te preocupes.

A echo
B hecho

7. ... una siesta y luego voy a verte.

A Echo
B Hecho

8. ¿Por qué no me has ... caso?

A hecho
B hechado

Tema The verb *caber*

Select the correct translation for each sentence.

Answers page 300

1. I don't fit into this suit.

A No cabo en este traje.

B No quepo en este traje.

2. We can't fit four people in this car.

A No cabemos cuatro en este coche.

B No quepamos cuatro en este coche.

3. This chair will never fit in the living room.

A Este sillón no cabrá nunca en el salón.

B Este sillón no cuprá nunca en el salón.

4. His shoes didn't fit in the closet.

A Sus zapatos no cupieron en el armario.

B Sus zapatos no cabieron en el armario.

5. Don't have the slightest doubt.

   A No te cabe la menor duda.

   B No te quepa la menor duda.

6. I don't think that the suitcases will fit.

   A No creo que quepan las maletas.

   B No creo que cupan las maletas.

Tema **Expressing a hypothetical situation in the past**

Choose the pair of verbs that make sense in the context. More than one response may be possible.

Answers page 300

1. Si ... descansado, ahora no ... sueño.

   A habías / tendrías   B hubieras / tendrías

   C hayas / tendrás   D habrías / tuvieras

2. Si no ... encendido un fuego, no ... habido un incendio.

   A hayáis / hubiera   B hubierais / habría

   C hubierais / hubiera   D habíais / hayáis

3. Si ... llegado antes al albergue, ... tenido una cama.

   A hubieran / habrían   B hubieran / hubieran

   C habrían / hubieran   D habían / habían

4. Si ... veraneado en la playa, ahora ... tomando el sol.

   A habríamos / estaríamos   B hubiéramos / estábamos

   C habríamos / estuviéramos D hubiéramos / estaríamos

5. Si me ... escuchado, no nos ... equivocado de camino.

   A hubieras / hubiéramos   B habrías / hubiéramos

   C hayas / habíamos   D hubieras / habríamos

6. Si no ... llovido, ya ... llegado.

   A hubiese / habríamos   B hubiera / habríamos

   C hubiese / hubiéramos   D hubiera / hubiéramos

anecer	*to begin to get light* (**Amanece.** *It's getting light. Day is breaking.*), *to wake up in the morning* (**Amanezco cansado.** *I wake up tired.*)
bucear	*to dive, to practise diving*
caber	*to fit* (in a space) (irregular in some persons and tenses, e.g. **quepo** *I fit*)
echar de menos	*to miss* (someone or something) (**echar una mano** *to give a hand*, **echar una peli** *to show a film*, **echar una siesta** *to have a nap*)
encender	*to light, to ignite* (verb with a spelling change)
escalar	*to scale, to climb*
hacer caso	*to listen, to pay attention*
helar	*to freeze* (verb with a spelling change)
jugar	*to play (a game)* (verb with a spelling change)
llover	*to rain* (verb with a spelling change)
nadar	*to swim*
nevar	*to snow* (verb with a spelling change)
persistir	*to persist, to continue*
pescar	*to fish*
practicar	*to practise*
prever	*to forecast, to anticipate*
saltar	*to jump, to leap*
ponerse	*to set, to go down* (the Sun)
soplar	*to blow*
veranear	*to spend the summer*

Geography vocabulary

el árbol	*tree*
la arena	*sand*

el bosque	*forest, wood*
el campo	*countryside*
el cielo	*sky*
la estrella	*star*
la hierba	*grass*
la isla	*island*
el lago	*lake*
la luna	*moon*
el monte	*mountain*
el océano	*ocean*
la orilla	*edge, bank, shore*
la playa	*beach*
el río	*river*

Weather words

caluroso	*hot, warm*
cubierto	*overcast*
despejado	*clear, cloudless*
helado	*frozen*
lluvioso	*rainy*
nevado	*snowy*
la nube	*cloud*
nublado	*cloudy*
soleado	*sunny*
templado	*temperate, mild*
el viento	*wind*
ventoso	*windy*

and physical activities
2**B** 3**A** 4**C** 5**B** 6**A** 7**B** 8**A** 9**C** 10**A**
A 2**B** 3**A** 4**D** 5**D** 6**C** 7**C** 8**B**

PAGE 291
Geography and landscapes
1**A** 2**D** 3**C** 4**B**
1**G** 2**C** 3**F** 4**B** 5**D** 6**H** 7**A** 8**E**
1**D** 2**F** 3**G** 4**B** 5**A** 6**E** 7**C** 8**H**

PAGE 294
The weather
1**B** 2**A** 3**A** 4**B** 5**A** 6**B** 7**B** 8**A** 9**A** 10**B**

PAGE 295
Whatever, wherever, whenever, whoever, however ...
1**D** 2**C** 3**B** 4**E** 5**A**

Hacer or *echar*?
1**B** 2**A** 3**A** 4**A** 5**A** 6**B** 7**A** 8**A**

PAGE 296
The verb *caber*
1**B** 2**A** 3**A** 4**A** 5**B** 6**A**

PAGE 297
Expressing a hypothetical situation in the past
1**B** 2**B**, **C** 3**A**, **B** 4**D** 5**A**, **D** 6**A**, **B**, **C**, **D**

YOUR SCORE:

Did you get between 0 and 14? ¡Ay, ay, ay!

Did you get between 15 and 29? Muy justito...

Did you get between 30 and 44? No está mal, pero...

Did you get between 45 and 59? Enhorabuena.

Did you get 60 or over? ¡Eres un auténtico fenómeno!

© 2020 Assimil
Legal deposit: September 2020
Publication number: 4012
ISBN: 9782700508802

Printed in Romania by
Tipografia Real

www.assimil.com